10 NOV 1988

13 JAN 1993

-5 FEB 1993

15 NOV 1993

-7 MAR 1994

-2 AUG 1996

2 6 SEP 2005

A GUIDE TO
CONGREGATIONAL AFFAIRS

A Guide to Congregational Affairs

ANDREW HERRON

THE SAINT ANDREW PRESS
EDINBURGH

First published in 1978 by
THE SAINT ANDREW PRESS
121 George Street, Edinburgh

© Andrew Herron 1978

ISBN 0 7152 0390 8

Printed and bound in Great Britain by
T. & A. Constable Ltd, Edinburgh

Contents

Preface

From time to time I am invited to conferences of office-bearers in different parts of the country. A suggestion frequently heard at such gatherings is that there is urgent need for a booklet explaining for the benefit of those responsible for the running of congregations something about how our Kirk works. Other requirements are that it should not be very long, not too complicated nor too dry, and that it shouldn't cost overmuch.

The following pages represent an attempt to supply this demand, and that on the terms stated.

It covers the main aspects in the life of a congregation in which office-bearers are especially involved: spiritual oversight, temporal management, and the filling of a vacancy, including the complication of readjustment.

It sets it forth very simply. This, of course, can be done only at the expense of accuracy and adequacy. For the profound student of church law Cox[1] is available, and with Cox I have neither desire nor ability to compete. This booklet is not meant to provide solutions for

[1] *Practice and Procedure in the Church of Scotland.* Edited by J.T. Cox. Sixth (1976) Edition, edited by D. F. M. Macdonald. Published by The Committee on General Administration of the Church of Scotland.

complex ecclesiastical problems but merely to help the ordinary church member to understand a little more clearly what it's all about.

It is, I hope, readable. Repeatedly this has led me to advance views that are purely personal and to make observations and give illustrations which purists may think irrelevant. My own hope is that these may result in the book being a human document; and if so I'll be very content, for the Kirk is all about people.

Thanks to the efforts of the Saint Andrew Press the booklet will be available at a price which, if not cheap by the standards of five years ago, will compare mighty favourably with the cost of the average paperback today.

So I would wish you bargain buying, relaxing reading, and happy hunting thereafter.

Glasgow 1978   ANDREW HERRON

1

The Kirk Session

The court upon whose shoulders lies the responsibility for the spiritual oversight of the parish is the Kirk Session. There is a Kirk Session in every parish in Scotland, and since every corner of Scotland lies within a parish it follows that every person resident in this country is the responsibility of some Kirk Session.

1. What is it?

The Kirk Session is made up of a minister (or ministers) and elders. Historically all are alike elders, being distinguished as respectively teaching (or preaching) elders and ruling elders, but general usage today confines the term 'elder' exclusively to the ruling variety. One sometimes hears the expression 'lay elder' but this, of course, is quite erroneous and even nonsensical — for there can be no such thing.

The Minister There has always to be a minister and he has to act as moderator. He is normally the minister of the parish; in a vacancy or during a period while the minister has been granted leave of absence there will be

an interim moderator appointed by the Presbytery; in the temporary absence of the minister or the interim moderator a moderator *pro
tempore* may be appointed by the regular
moderator. In the case of a collegiate charge
both ministers are members of Session and
take turns in the moderatorial chair. A retired
minister, or a minister employed extra-
parochially may be associated with the pastoral
work of a Kirk Session, but so long as he retains
his status as a minister he will not be a member
of it.

The Elders   These are those members of a
congregation who have been ordained as
elders and have been admitted as members of
that particular Kirk Session. Thus while it is
true to say 'once an elder always an elder' this
must not be taken to imply that an elder will
always be a member of Kirk Session. In the
absence of a minister as moderator the elders
can meet in an unofficial way but cannot
constitute themselves a Kirk Session.

'Minister and Kirk Session'   This is a phrase
sometimes come across in official documents
such as a petition to, or an order from, the
General Assembly. The phrase may be ob-
jected to as tautologous on the ground that the
reference to the minister is duplicated. This is
true, but the phrase is correct, for the minister
is appearing in two different roles and in these
his interest need not necessarily be identical;
there could well be a conflict of interest as a
result of which the minister in his capacity as
minister of the parish held a view completely at

variance with that of all or a majority of the elders.

2. How are its members selected?

Adding to its Number   The number of elders is decided by the Kirk Session, which also decides when it is expedient to add to its number, and which, in the last resort, determines who shall be added. The Presbytery has a responsibility, however, to ensure that the number of elders does not fall below what in its opinion is an adequate strength. Where (as a result, for example, of a mass resignation) the number of elders falls to a level at which the Kirk Session cannot function a problem obviously arises. For the only way to replenish its strength is to meet and resolve to add new elders; but if a quorum cannot be found there can be no meeting. A way out of this *impasse* is found by the presbytery appointing 'assessors' to sit with the Kirk Session till steps can be taken to add new elders and have an enlarged Kirk Session constituted in the regular way. Such assessors are members of Presbytery and may be either elders or ministers. In the early stages of the life of a Church Extension charge assessor elders are appointed by the Presbytery and these are elders from neighbouring Kirk Sessions.

Eligibility   To be eligible for membership of the Kirk Session a person must be in full communion with the church, must be a member of that congregation, must be at least twenty-one years of age, and may be either male or female. In terms of an 18th century Act he should be 'of good life and godly conversation, tender and circumspect in his walk, punctual in attending on ordinances, strict in his observance of the Lord's Day, and keeping up the worship of God in his family; and one who will be careful of the flock, an example of sobriety, meekness, holiness, abstaining from all appearance of evil'.

There are practical considerations affecting the advisability of a paid servant of the Kirk Session (organist, beadle, etc) being a member of the court, but there is no law forbidding it.

Method of Choice The new elders may be chosen in any one of three ways, and the decision as to which of these will be followed lies with the Session itself.

(*a*) *Congregational Meeting* After two Sundays' intimation a meeting of the congregation is held at which nominations are called for. Let it be that six is the number to be added. It may be agreed once six nominations have been received that this is adequate, in which case a vote For or Against the election of these six is to be taken. Clearly this is not necessarily a very satisfactory method since it involves as the criterion of selection speed of nomination rather than degree of popular support. It may therefore be deemed wise to go on and accept further nominations. When it is clear that no further names are forthcoming the vote is taken. Let it be that nine names have been received. Incidentally, it is rather important that, if at all possible, the number received should exceed the number required by more than one, or even two. Otherwise the one person not elected becomes rather conspicuous.

The vote is taken either by standing up or by the use of voting papers. If the former method is followed each member has, in our hypothetical case, six votes, and the procedure is simple and straightforward. The nine names are read out, it is explained that each member has a maximum of six votes to cast, tellers are appointed, and the names are put up and voted on one after the other. If, on the other hand, the meeting resolves that voting papers are to be used the Session must arrange for the printing of such papers setting forth the names of the nominees in alphabetical order, and must also arrange for these to be distributed to the members with a closing date for their return. In either case the six nominees having secured the highest number of votes are then declared to have been elected, subject to the judgment of the Kirk Session. For it is still for the Kirk Session to satisfy itself as to the suitability of the persons elected. It must be obvious that, unless for the most compelling reason, it is near impossible for the Kirk Session at this stage to do other than acquiesce in the result of the voting.

(b) *Signed Lists* The congregation may be invited by pulpit intimation to submit, not later than a specified date, signed lists containing names up to the number required. After the expiry of the allotted time the Session meets and counts up the results and those with the highest number of 'appearances' are declared to be elected, subject, as above, to the judgment of the Kirk Session.

(c) *Kirk Session Resolution*   The Session itself may make choice of eligible persons whom it deems suitable. This method has the advantage that consideration may be given to the suitability of each person proposed within the confidentiality of the Session meeting. It also avoids the kind of situation that can arise where a person elected in public is not acceptable to the Session. If this method is to be adopted there is nothing to prevent the Session inviting the congregation to assist by submitting suggestions in writing for their consideration, though care must be taken if this is done that there is no confusion with (b) above.

Consent   If the method of open election is followed it will be usual for the person nominated to have been present and his consent taken or assumed at the time. In the other two cases, though, no such assumption may be made. It is usual for the minister, accompanied perhaps by the Session Clerk or by the elder of the district, to visit the person proposed and gain his consent. Where there are a few such calls to be made they should be carried out as nearly simultaneously as possible to avoid the impression that those visited after a lapse of some days have been 'second choices', with unfortunate results. Letters sent to all at the same time avoid this danger, but they are a poor substitute for a personal approach and in my view are to be discouraged.

Edict An edict is then served on two Sundays, setting forth the names and designations of the persons chosen and appointing a meeting of the Kirk Session at which any person wishing to do so may appear to object to the life or doctrine of any of those named. Customarily this meeting is timed for half-an-hour or so before the Service of Admission. It is stipulated in the edict that unless objection be lodged 'and immediately substantiated' the ordination or admission will proceed as arranged. This does not mean that the objector must come prepared fully to prove his case at that Session meeting; but two things are essential, first that the allegation is such as, if proved, would be fatal to the person's admission to the Session; and secondly that it be backed up by that degree of evidence that will establish a *prima facie* case. It should be noted that objection must be to life or doctrine. It would seem to follow that an objection based upon suitability or adequacy could not be upheld. (While formal objections at this stage are thus strictly confined, it is my opinion that at the point when the Kirk Session reached its decision — before, that is, the edict had been read — it was not thus strictly confined.) In order to establish an interest to intervene the objector should be either a member or a parishioner; he need not be both. In advancing his objection he is protected by a fair degree of privilege and an action of defamation would not lie provided his objection was *bona fide* (not malicious) and was supported by a measure of probability. In a case within my own knowledge substantial damages were awarded against members who canvassed a paper of objection around householders in the parish, this being regarded as vastly different from personally appearing before the Session with an objection.

Service of Admission   Elders are admitted at a Service of Public Worship when those becoming elders for the first time are ordained, and all are admitted to the membership of the Kirk Session. All alike are asked to assent to the prescribed questions and to sign the Formula. In the Service of Ordination there is no laying on of hands as with ministers. All present members of Session take part in the giving of the right hand of fellowship to the new elders. It is a considerable advantage to have a copy of the Formula written on, or pasted into, the back page of the Session minute-book, or in a separate volume, and to enter the date each time fresh signatures are added. This, of course, in addition to the normal minute recording the event in the body of the volume.

I have on occasion been asked whether admission in face of the congregation is absolutely essential in every case. When, for example, a member of Session who had left the district and has now returned and rejoined the congregation could not he be quietly restored to his erstwhile position by a simple resolution of Kirk Session? I am sure there must be an edict and an opportunity for objection, but for my own part I can see no good reason why in such a case the actual admission should not take place at a Session meeting, provided the questions are asked and the Formula signed. I think, though, that unless in quite exceptional circumstances it is better that the full regular procedure should be followed.

Length of Tenure On transferring to another congregation an elder automatically ceases to be a member of his former Kirk Session. Each elder is subject to the discipline of his own Kirk Session which, on sufficient cause, may suspend him from office. The fact that he may be a 'Presbytery Elder' does nothing to alter this relationship. Where an elder has been absent from Session meetings for the space of one year without sufficient reason known it is open to the Kirk Session to find that he is no longer of their number, though this of itself does not deprive him of his status as an elder.

3. Who are its officials?

The Moderator A minister, immediately on his induction to a parish, becomes *ex officio* moderator of its Kirk Session. He is furnished by the Presbytery Clerk with a record of his induction, and this he should present at the first Session meeting and the fact should be recorded in the minute. As explained above, his place as moderator may be taken on occasion, but only by another minister. Where there is a collegiate ministry the ministers take turns of presiding, the one who is not in the chair sitting and voting as the other elders. In the case of an associate ministry the minister is the only Moderator of Session, the associate sitting and voting as an elder. An ordained assistant though he has a seat in Presbytery has no place on the Kirk Session, but he may be invited to attend its meetings. It is recommended that a deaconess should be so invited to attend meetings of the Kirk Session of the parish where she is working. She may, of course, be an elder and as such be admitted to the Kirk Session. The same considerations apply in the case of a lay missionary.

The moderator has a casting vote only, but he may introduce business to the Kirk Session and he may speak to any item of business that is before the court. He has also the right to dissent from a decision of the Kirk Session and to complain to the Presbytery. He may leave the chair if he feels this will save embarrassment in the discussion of some item in which he has a personal interest, but he must resume the chair before any decisions are reached on the matter.

It is the responsibility of the moderator to convene meetings of the Kirk Session. This may in fact be done by the clerk, but if so it is done under authority of the moderator. (For further particulars about the calling of meetings see p. 13.) The moderator presides at all meetings, opening and closing them with prayer. He keeps good order, puts issues to the vote and announces the decision, and he ensures that a proper record of the proceedings is kept.

The moderator is as completely bound as is any other member of the congregation by decisions of the Kirk Session, the significant difference being that while the Session itself normally deals with cases of disobedience, in the case of the moderator it is only the Presbytery that can judge of his conduct.

Session Clerk A clerk is appointed by the Kirk Session and holds office during its pleasure. On his taking up his duties he takes the oath *de fideli* ('I promise to carry out faithfully the duties of Session Clerk.') It is his duty to take regular minutes and to engross them in a permanent record, to keep Session documents, and, when so authorised, to issue extracts of Session minutes. In his absence a clerk *pro tempore* may be appointed, and he should take the oath. In the continuing absence of a clerk it is the duty of the moderator to keep the record, which he does as 'moderator and clerk'. This is a quite unsatisfactory state of affairs which should not be allowed to continue longer than can possibly be avoided. It is in order, and may sometimes prove advantageous, to appoint a clerk who is not a member of the court. It is unusual for the clerk to receive payment for his services, though in some cases where considerable work is involved a modest honorarium is paid.

A question is often asked about the admissibility of keeping Session minutes in the form of a loose-leaf record. Traditionally the church has frowned upon such practices. For myself I see this as playing Canute to the tide. The loose-leaf record has come to stay, and the copper-plate writer has gone. In such circumstances there is much to be said in favour of minutes neatly typed on separate sheets. The main requirements for a record are that it should be permanent and that its contents should be trustworthy. The former demands that at some point the loose leaves shall be bound into a permanent volume, and the latter requires that while they are still loose sheets the minutes shall be authenticated with the signatures of moderator and clerk on each sheet — otherwise it would be very easy for some unscrupulous person to substitute a sheet altered in some material particular. Until they are bound into a volume the loose-leaf minutes present the Session Clerk with a considerable responsibility.

The General Assembly has required that all Session records of date prior to 1900 should be passed to the Principal Clerk for transmission to Register House where all church records are preserved on permanent loan.

Treasurer There are generally certain funds falling to be administered by the Kirk Session: Benevolent Fund, certain bequest funds left in the control of the Session; a Treasurer should be appointed to take charge of these. There is nothing to prevent the Session Treasurer being the same person who acts as Kirk Treasurer, but in such a case care should be taken that account is given to the

Session alone for the funds that are their
business.

Officer In common with other courts the
Session should have an officer to wait on its
meetings and to execute its orders. The Session
Officer will normally be the same person as the
Church Officer, commonly referred to, in the
country at least, as 'the beadle'.

4. How does it meet?

Regular Meetings It is common, particularly
in larger congregations, for there to be regular
meetings of the Kirk Session, on the third
Wednesday of each month, or what-have-you.
These are often incorrectly referred to as
'statutory meetings', a name properly to be
applied only to a meeting held in consequence
of some order of a superior court. The proper
title is 'regular' or 'monthly' meetings. There is,
in fact, no obligation to hold regular meetings
or indeed to meet at all except insofar as it is
required that the Session should meet within two months of the close of the General
Assembly each year to appoint a representative
elder to Presbytery and Synod.

Convening of Meetings Meetings are properly convened either by pulpit intimation or by
personal notice given to each member. When
the Kirk Session includes assessors from other
congregations, pulpit intimation must be sup-
plemented by personal notice to all such
assessors. Unless for the transaction of some
quite formal item of business, a meeting should

not be held at the close of the service at which it was first intimated. Notice calling a Session meeting must be 'timeous' though what constitutes such notice may well vary from one parish to another. Two Sundays' pulpit intimation, or not less than seven clear days after receipt of the personal notice, would seem to me to be free from challenge. Less than that I should think doubtful if matters of importance are to be on the agenda.

Requisition   When required in writing by at least one-third of the elders (not less than five if there are more than nine) the moderator must call a meeting within ten days. This provision is written into the Basis of Union of 1929, but it is not made clear whether the ten days' limit applies to the calling or to the holding of the meeting. I incline to think it must be the calling. Let it be that a minister is handed a writing at the close of public worship on a Sunday. Pulpit intimation could not be made before the following Sunday and if the meeting had to be within ten days it would need to be on the Tuesday at the latest, forty-eight hours away. This would seem to me to be inadequate notice and would to that extent defeat the purpose of the requisition. I think the law will be fulfilled if the meeting is called within ten days and held as soon as conveniently possible thereafter.

If the writing disclose that the business for which the meeting is being requisitioned is incompetent the moderator is not obliged to comply. I take it that the test of competence is the same as the moderator would apply were

the matter raised in the course of a regular
Session meeting. Should the moderator refuse
or fail to call a meeting after being requisitioned to do so in due form the matter may
be made the subject of petition to the Presbytery in name of the requisitioning elders.
Should it be that the moderator's ruling on
competence was considered faulty I am of the
opinion that the matter could be challenged at
the next regular meeting of Session and ap-
pealed from there to the Presbytery, or that it
could be made the subject of direct petition to
the Presbytery without waiting till the Session
had met.

Agenda   For practical reasons there is considerable advantage in having an agenda prepared in advance of each regular Session
meeting. A copy of this may be sent out with the
notice calling the meeting, or copies may be
circulated at the meeting, or its items may be
read out at an early stage in the proceedings. It
should be made clear that anyone wishing to
raise some matter not included must at that
point secure a place on the agenda 'or remain
forever silent'. The inclusion at the end of the
agenda of an item 'Any other competent
business' is, from the point of view of good
order, to be sternly discouraged.

Quorum   Irrespective of the size of the Kirk
Session the quorum is three, of whom, of
course, one must be the moderator.

Constitution   Practice varies considerably as
to the precise form of the opening devotions at
a Session meeting. It is obligatory if the court is

to be legally constituted that it should be
'opened with prayer' and that this fact should
be recorded in the minute. Any extract from
the minutes should begin with a reference to
this fact — 'At . . . on . . . the Kirk Session of . . .
met and was constituted.' The meeting must
also be closed with prayer, though in ordinary
circumstances this is now accepted as meaning
'with the benediction'.

Minutes   After the meeting has been constituted and the sederunt taken the minutes of
the previous meeting or meetings should be
read, though if copies have been circulated in
advance they may be 'taken as read'. They
should then be approved or, if need be,
adjusted, and with the authority of the court
signed by the moderator and clerk. They
should never be signed in advance by either
official, nor should they be left to be signed at
some later date. It is the moderator and clerk
acting at the time when the minutes are
approved who sign, not those acting at the
meeting of which the minute is the record. Any
material alteration in a minute should be
initialled by both moderator and clerk; a literal
correction may be authenticated by the clerk
alone. The minute which records the approval
of the earlier minute should also record any
material alteration that has been made in it
('Minutes of . . . were approved, subject to the
deletion in line . . . on page . . . of the words . . .
and to the addition at the end of the following
line of the words . . .'.) It should always be
borne in mind that the approval of the minute

implies merely its acceptance as an accurate historical account of what happened and does not involve the approval of what was done. Even if what was done was completely out of order it has to be recorded as having been done, if for no other purpose than to allow steps to be taken to rectify the irregularity.

Standing Orders   It is always open to a court to make Standing Orders to regulate its methods of procedure and to hold itself bound by these unless their suspension has been agreed, usually only on a two-thirds majority. But it is not, in my experience, common for Kirk Sessions to have Standing Orders, and in such circumstances the Session is held to be bound by those of the next superior court, the Presbytery.

Meetings are Private   Unlike the other courts of the Church the Kirk Session normally meets in private and its business is therefore confidential. There are many matters that come before the present-day Kirk Session where confidentiality is not really necessary, but unless it has been resolved otherwise the ban on disclosure stands. And in such fields as, for example, discipline, the greatest circumspection is necessary. It may be that in the early stages of discussion with representatives of the Presbytery in regard to readjustment, nothing but harm can result from disclosure of plans in which the interests of other parties are involved before it has been possible to confer with these parties. After all, you can't start everywhere at once! The utmost confidentiality should therefore be observed. If the whole business of the Session is treated as confidential (as it is) there is less chance of curiosity being evoked when an elder declines to comment upon some particular item.

5. What does it do?

An Act of 1931 lays it down that 'it is the duty of the Kirk Session to maintain good order, to cause Acts of Assembly to be put into execution, to administer discipline, to judge and determine causes, and to superintend the religious and moral condition of the parish.' This might well be put more simply by stating that the Kirk Session is responsible for the spiritual oversight of its parish.

For our present purpose it might be more convenient to say that the Kirk Session has a responsibility (a) for the people of the parish, (b) for the services of the sanctuary, (c) for the organisations of the congregation, and (d) for overseeing the conduct of a vacancy. I shall try to detail their duties under these four heads.

Care of the People

In a strict sense the Kirk Session has a duty of care towards all the people of the parish, though in practice today the Session has little opportunity of extending this care beyond the actual members of the congregation and their families. The break-up of the traditional parish, the growth of denominations, the increase of those not interested even nominally in the church, have all played a part in making it difficult for the Session to exercise that degree of spiritual oversight that traditionally and constitutionally is its duty.

Elders' Districts   To most elders is entrusted the care of a district and they are supplied with a book showing the names and addresses of all members of the congregation residing therein. At the lowest estimate their duty is to deliver Communion Cards in these homes at the appropriate times. Responsible elders will see themselves as having a duty also to take a personal interest in those committed to their care. They should concern themselves not only with the members but with the families of the members and should seek to direct young people into involvement in the life of the congregation. When members move house the elder should not be content to return the card marked 'Gone Away' but should make it his business to find precisely where they have gone. From time to time the Assembly passes resolutions about the proper reaction to those who move out of the parish. Clearly that duty can be fulfilled only if their new address is known. Enquiries made of neighbours at or about the time of removal will usually elicit this information; it can be nearly impossible to obtain it later.

When the elder's district lies within the parish he has a special duty to keep himself informed about all that is happening, and in particular to inform himself (and his minister) of the arrival of people who should be in the congregation.

Elders can be of enormous service by reporting immediately to the minister for his attention cases of sickness, of complaints, etc., discovered on their rounds.

Keeping of Communion Roll This duty is laid upon the Kirk Session by Act vi of 1938 which has subsequently been amended. A Roll is to be kept showing the names and addresses of all members of the congregation, indicating when and how they joined and when and how they departed, and giving a record also of their attendance at Communion. For the latter purpose card-index or loose-leaf sheets are most convenient, but the other information should be available somewhere in permanent form.

Transference Certificates The Session is responsible for issuing and receiving Certificates of Transference, and particular care should be taken when such a certificate is issued to a member to ensure that the Advice Notice is forwarded to the minister of the congregation to which he or she is going or, if that is not known, to the Presbytery Clerk for transmission to the minister of the parish. When members are given certificates on leaving the district it should be impressed upon them that they must lodge these without delay. It is no uncommon thing for someone to produce a certificate anything up to twenty years old but in mint condition, happily assuring you that, of course, he's got his 'lines' all right. Anything that can be done to discourage the almost superstitious reverence for 'my church lines' is well worth doing.

An Act of 1977 reduces the period of validity of a Transference Certificate to one year and requires that a Session may accept an out-of-date certificate only after 'investigating the circumstances carefully' and taking 'such other action as it shall deem appropriate'.

Revision of Communion Roll Towards the close of each calendar year the Roll should be revised and attested, and this fact should be recorded in the Session minutes. At this annual revision the Session is entitled to remove from the Roll the names of those who are not showing interest or involvement in the work of the congregation. It is presumably for the Session to determine what constitutes taking a sufficient interest in the work of the congregation, but once having decided that someone falls short of the standard the Session is required to raise with him personally 'the question of adherence to vows of Church membership'. The matter is no longer bound up with absence from Communion for three years, but consistent abstention from the Lord's Table must in ordinary circumstances be seen as evidence of lack of interest. Once a name has been removed in this way it can be restored only by resolution of Kirk Session.

Supplementary Roll A Supplementary Roll is also to be kept, and to this is to be transferred any name taken from the Communion Roll in terms of the foregoing paragraph where the person concerned continues to reside in the parish. Two things should be noted: first, that the appearance of a person's name on the Supplementary Roll does not confer any rights whatever on that person; and secondly, that this Roll should be used exclusively for those resident within the parish. It is my experience that the uses to which the Supplementary Roll is put are many and varied. I am not myself satisfied that it fulfils any very useful purpose. In a large city parish it is never easy to keep track of the movements of those on the Communion Roll proper; how much more difficult for those on the Supplementary Roll. And in a small country community they are well enough known without needing to have their names engrossed on a Roll. But the Act requires that such a Roll shall be kept.

Minister's Name   Sometimes the question is asked whether the name of the minister should appear on the Communion Roll since he is not answerable to the Kirk Session. I am quite clear in my own mind that it should. The Roll is primarily a list of people entitled to take Communion, not a list of those who are subject to the discipline of the Session.

Admission to Communion   This is the direct responsibility of the Kirk Session, no matter through which of the three possible doors the person is entering the fellowship of the congregation.

(*a*) *By Profession*   The training of communicants is the affair of the minister, but it is the duty of the Kirk Session to satisfy itself as to their suitability, to hear their profession of faith, and to extend to them the right hand of fellowship.

(b) *By Certificate of Transference* It is for the Session to agree to the acceptance of Certificates of Transference from other congregations. When a Certificate bears a date of issue showing it to be more than a year old then, unless there be some special and adequate explanation, admission should be by method (c) hereunder. The Act of 1977 demands that a Certificate of Transference be automatically issued to anyone leaving the district and that the name of such a person be continued on the Roll only on a specific resolution to that effect.

(c) *By Resolution of Kirk Session* When a person has already made profession of faith but for some reason has lapsed from membership it lies within the discretion of the Kirk Session to resolve that his name should be restored to the Communion Roll.

Removal from Roll Names are removed from the Roll (a) by Death. (b) by Certificate of Transference, and (c) at the annual revision as described above. It is only the last of these which requires an act of the Kirk Session.

Discipline The Kirk Session of an earlier generation was much engaged in the exercise of discipline, they took very seriously their involvement in the moral condition of the parish. Today where scandal exists it is usual for the matter to be left to the minister who will seek by admonition and exhortation to effect some betterment. It has always to be borne in mind that the blessings of the faith are not meant to be a reward for the 'unco guid' but are intended to be a help to the sinner, and that driving people out of the fellowship on the occasion of a moral lapse is not a Christian response.

Benevolent Fund   Another survival from an earlier day is the responsibility of the Kirk Session for the care of the poor of the parish. Time was when the church was the only body in the land recognising a duty towards the poor; today this whole department has been taken over by the State (to which it properly belongs) and increasingly the administration of what funds of this sort still exist is being handed over to the financial court. While, however, you may hand over authority you cannot divest yourself of responsibility and it should be borne in mind that the responsibility here rests squarely with the Kirk Session.

There are certain sums which by the law of the land are payable to the Kirk Session for the benefit of the poor: (*a*) gambling winnings exceeding one hundred merks in twenty-four hours (by an Act of 1621), (*b*) fines for profaneness and Sabbath profanation, and (*c*) fines and forfeitures under the Day Poaching Act of 1832. I do not imagine that today prosecutions are being brought under the first two of these statutes, and most poaching seems to be pursued in the hours of darkness! So the income is negligible. A number of years ago, though, I received as parish minister the sale-price of a poacher's nets forfeited under the Act (from the price I presumed they had not been very good nets!) It should be emphasised that such sums are for the poor of the parish, that is to say, parishioners unconnected with the congregation qualify, while members who live outwith the parish, however deserving, do not.

Congregational Meeting Most congregational meetings are called for temporal purposes (like authorising the sale of property) but from time to time issues will arise that are not wholly of this character and that require to be submitted to the congregation. In such circumstances a meeting is required for ecclesiastical purposes. Such a meeting is called by authority of the Kirk Session, requires two Sundays' notice giving an indication of the business to be transacted, is presided over by the Moderator of Session, and a record of the business is kept by the Session Clerk and entered in the Session minute-book. Special rules apply in the case of meetings in connection with readjustment (see p. 101).

Services of the Sanctuary

'It belongs to the Kirk Session in concurrence with the Minister to regulate the hours of public worship and to fix the number of Church services. The Kirk Session may appoint such occasional or special services as it judges desirable.' I am not myself very clear as to what the position would be were the 'concurrence' to be lacking. I incline to the view that

the Kirk Session has the last word as to the
number of services and the hours at which they
shall be held. It would follow that it would be in
order, for example, for the Session to decide
that there should be two services each Sunday,
at 11 and 6.30, and should so decide in spite of
the minister's insistence that he would rather
be doing something informal with youth at the
evening hour. Since the actual conduct of the
service lies completely outwith the control of
the Session it is not easy to see what effective
action the elders can take without ministerial
concurrence if, for instance, the minister fails
to appear at 6.30. A petition to Presbytery in
name of the Kirk Session would seem to be the
appropriate remedy. Or if the presence of the
minister as Moderator of Session made this
difficult the elders as a group of individuals
could institute such a petition.

All matters affecting the actual conduct of
public worship and the administering of the
sacraments are the affair of the Presbytery.
Yes, please note, of the Presbytery. The elders
have no say whatever. 'In those things the Kirk
Session has no authority and the elders are
even as other members of the congregation as
regards power and authority.'[1] While it is the
Presbytery that has authority, the executive
officer of the Presbytery is the minister. The
minister, then, is not, as is sometimes represented, his own master in all matters affecting the conduct of the services. He is very much

[1] *Digest of Church Laws* by W. Mair.

responsible to the Presbytery since everything he does in this field is done in its name.

Two further points are worth noting in this connection. First that though the Kirk Session has no authority for the conduct of public worship there is no reason why the minister should not consult with the Session and consider the opinions of the members on any proposal, especially if it is to alter the traditional pattern of worship while, of course, ensuring that the matter is not so recorded in the minute as to convey the impression that a decision of Session had been reached on the subject. And, secondly, that any member of the congregation dissatisfied with the minister's conduct of worship and unable to get satisfaction from him must go to the Presbytery by petition; the Kirk Session can do nothing for him.

Communion   The elders assist the minister in the distribution of the elements at Communion. This they do in their individual capacity as elders and not corporately as the Kirk Session. There is therefore no need for the Kirk Session to be constituted for the celebration of the sacrament though it may well have been constituted for the purpose of receiving communicants and there is no reason why it should not continue in session. The tradition that the elders help in this way is so well established that it is difficult to imagine a congregational Communion service where any other arrangement obtained; but at a special service there is no obligation upon the minister to use the services of the elders even if these are available; a Woman's Guild dedication service, for example, might very properly involve the distribution of the elements by members of the Guild who were not elders.

Organist The organist (or precentor, or leader of praise) is appointed and dismissed by the Kirk Session which, before it appoints him, has to be satisfied as to his Christian character. His salary is fixed and paid by the financial court. In all matters affecting public worship he is under the direction and control of the minister. The extent of his duties, his right of access to the instrument, his claim to fees for special engagements, and other like matters should be incorporated in an agreement or contract between himself and the Kirk Session, accepted by him on his appointment, and a copy should be retained by each party. Psalmody committees and the like are purely advisory in character, and responsibility lies with the Kirk Session or with the minister as the case may be.

Church Officer The Church Officer is also appointed and dismissed by the Kirk Session. In his duties as Session Officer he takes his orders from the minister. As Church Officer and Hall-keeper he should have a written contract which, among other things, makes clear precisely to whom he is answerable. Nothing will more quickly or more surely lead to the loss of a good officer than a multiplicity of 'bosses'. The better the man the sooner he'll go under such conditions.

Congregational Organisations

All societies, associations, and organisations connected with the congregation are under supervision of the Kirk Session. This is true of all societies, even of those which have a central organisation of their own, such as the Boys' Brigade, the Girl Guides, etc. An organisation cannot be started in the congregation without the approval of the Kirk Session. The Sunday School in particular is under supervision of the Kirk Session which, because of its responsibility for the Christian instruction of youth, has a special interest. The minister is 'head' of the Sunday School (even when, as is usual, someone else acts as superintendent). Again there are here possibilities of a clash when differences of opinion arise between the minister as 'head' of the Sunday School, the elders as its 'supervisors', and the superintendent as its 'leader'. My own impression is that the minister would have the final word, but that the Kirk Session would have a duty, if they felt strongly enough on the issue, to reach a decision which was in conflict with the minister's; and on his indicating that he did not intend to follow it, it would be open to them to approach the Presbytery by petition.

It is a common, and a commendable, practice that an elder is (or a pair of elders are) designated to represent the Kirk Session on each of the organisations. In this way what can so easily be no more than a formal relationship can become a meaningful connection.

Use of Church Buildings   The church and

other ecclesiastical buildings are constantly at the disposal of the minister for the purposes of his office. This last phrase — for the purposes of his office — should be heavily underlined, for the buildings are not the minister's to do with as he will. He may, however, grant permission to use them for all purposes connected with the congregation and its organisations, and even for purposes unconnected with the congregation provided they are of a religious, ecclesiastical or charitable nature. For any other use the minister must have the consent of the responsible financial court, and that court, in turn, can grant use only with consent of minister and Kirk Session.

Church Bell   'To the minister belongs exclusively the power of regulating the time and manner of ringing the bell of the church in connection with ecclesiastical or religious purposes.'[1]

Vacancy Procedure

This whole subject is dealt with fully later (p. 105). For the present suffice it to say that the Kirk Session has an overall responsibility in connection with the filling of a vacancy, and has also a number of specific duties in this connection.

Electoral Register   It is the duty of the Kirk Session immediately permission to call has been given to prepare an Electoral Register for the congregation and to have it attested by the

---

[1] *Digest of Church Laws* by W. Mair.

Presbytery. It is for the Session to adjudicate upon applications to be added to the Register as adherents, and against a decision of Session on this point there is no right of appeal.

Pulpit Supply   It is for the Kirk Session, in consultation with the interim moderator, to make arrangements for the supply of the pulpit during the period of the vacancy.

Election of Minister   So soon as the Vacancy Committee has made its choice of a nominee, or nominees, it bows itself out from the scene and the Kirk Session takes over, arranging for the election of the minister and seeing, if appropriate, to the printing of ballot papers. The elders, along with the interim moderator, supervise the election, and if a ballot has been held, they see to the counting of the votes and the declaration of the result (p. 121).

Preparation of Call   It is also for the Kirk Session to arrange that a Call shall be prepared and opportunity provided for it to be signed. The Call may be made available for signature at various places within the parish, but an elder must always be present to witness the signing. An elder may add to the Call, and ratify with his initials, the name of someone who has submitted to the Session Clerk a duly completed form of mandate. It is expressly forbidden to canvass the Call from house to house.

The Kirk Session has also the duty of ensuring that all relevant papers are transmitted to the Presbytery Clerk.

6. To whom is it answerable?

With certain very precise and limited exceptions any matter coming regularly before a Kirk Session may be the subject of complaint to the Presbytery and thence to the Synod and the General Assembly. The Presbytery is the court to which the Kirk Session is immediately answerable. The Presbytery can at any time, for reason which it considers adequate, summon a meeting of Kirk Session or of congregation. The Session must not meet when the Presbytery is sitting.

Visitation of Records The Session minutebook, the Communion Roll, the Baptismal Register and the Property Register, as well as the minute-book of the financial court, have annually to be submitted for inspection by the Presbytery. All records of date prior to the turn of the century are to be forwarded to the Principal Clerk of Assembly, who will transmit them for safe custody to H.M. Keeper of Records at Register House. There they are constantly available for inspection. If it is desired that they should be retransmitted for a period for some specific purpose (a congregational exhibition, for example) application should be made through the Presbytery.

Quinquennial Visitation On the occasion of the quinquennial visitation of the congregation, the visiting committee holds a separate meeting with the Kirk Session and is entitled to meet with the elders in the absence of the minister.

Representative Elder Each Kirk Session, within two months of the close of the General Assembly each year, appoints an elder to represent it in Presbytery and Synod. Normally this will be one of its own number, but may be any *bona fide* acting elder within the bounds of the Presbytery. Elders' commissions run from 1st July to 30th June and may be presented and sustained at any meeting of Presbytery, ordinary or otherwise, held subsequently to the close of the General Assembly. Recent legislation has provided that in the case of a linked charge each Kirk Session shall appoint a representative elder. In the case of the death, resignation, or disqualification of the representative elder another may at the earliest opportunity be appointed in his place.

Assembly Representation Elders to attend the General Assembly are commissioned by Presbyteries, not by Kirk Sessions. Most Presbyteries, however, have a system by which each Kirk Session is given a turn (probably every fourth year) to nominate a *bona fide* acting elder who will subsequently be appointed by the Presbytery.

Matters Sent Down for Comment Occasionally matters that are before the General Assembly are sent down to Presbyteries and to Kirk Sessions for comment. In such a case copies of the relevant section of the Report will be supplied in sufficient numbers for each member, and a specific date will be indicated by which comments are to be returned. This is not to be confused in any way with Barrier Act procedure,[1] which is exclusively a reference to Presbyteries. It is different too from a recent practice of indicating a willingness to receive and consider opinions and comments from Kirk Sessions. In this case it is for any Session which wishes to do so to equip itself with copies of the report and to send their comments through the Presbytery.

There is no provision in the law or practice of the Church for a referendum going down to all members or for any matter to require the approval of a majority of Kirk Sessions.

[1] See *A Guide to the General Assembly* (Saint Andrew Press, 1976), p. 14.

2
Managing the Temporal Affairs

Within the Church of Scotland there is a wide
diversity among the methods employed for
managing the business side of the life of the
congregation, for 'the administration of its
temporal affairs' as it is officially described. In
general terms it can be said that the responsibility for this is carried by one or other of four
bodies: the Kirk Session, the Congregational
Board, the Deacons' Court, or the Committee
of Management. Again in general terms, these
methods are to be found respectively in old
Parish kirks, in Parishes *quoad sacra*, in former
Free Church congregations, and in congregations belonging to the United Presbyterian
tradition.

The method in vogue in any particular
congregation will depend upon the historical
background of that congregation. And for that
reason there may be some advantage in beginning with a brief historical survey. Even before
doing so, however, some of the terms that will
have to be used call for a word of simple
explanation.

1. Meaning of the terms used

Parish, Free, U.P.   It is generally recognised that the present Church of Scotland was created in 1929 by the union of the then Church of Scotland and the United Free Church of Scotland. That latter body in turn had come into existence as the result of the union in 1900 between the Free Church and the United Presbyterian Church. To go back a stage further, one recalls that the Free Church was born in 1843 when a considerable proportion of the membership of the Church of Scotland divided itself off (in the Disruption) to form a separate denomination. To this, in 1876, there attached itself the Reformed Presbyterian Church which had broken off from the parent stem as early as 1690. The United Presbyterian Church, on the other hand, represented the fusion in 1847 of the Secession Church (formed in 1733) with the Relief Church (formed in 1761). The three separate and quite distinct traditions which merged together in 1929 were, therefore, Parish, Free, and U.P.

Parishes Quoad Omnia *and Parishes* Quoad Sacra   When the first elementary patterns of local government emerged in Scotland the legislators naturally enough accepted the existing ecclesiastical division of the country into parishes. Parish Councils took care of poor relief, Parish School Boards looked after education, and so on, always within the area represented by a parish with its Parish Kirk.

What had in the first place been a territorial division for purely ecclesiastical purposes thus came to provide a unit for a variety of civil purposes.

The enormous movement of population that resulted from the Industrial Revolution confronted the national church with many problems. Vast communities of people were far from their parish kirk, far indeed from any kirk. It was therefore necessary to establish new charges, to erect new buildings, to carve out new parishes, if these people were to be cared for. So the Kirk set about its first Church Extension programme.

The civil authorities, however, did not follow these new patterns but continued their administration according to the old divisions. To take a specific example, the town of Barrhead grew up within the parish of Neilston which, ere long, it vastly overshadowed in size and importance if not physically. Although it came to have its own church its civil affairs were still those of the larger unit of Neilston, and that although the executive office may well have been in Barrhead. Barrhead, then, being a parish exclusively from the point of view of the church came to be known as a 'parish *quoad sacra*' (in respect of religious affairs) whereas Neilston was a 'parish *quoad omnia*' (in respect of all affairs). It should perhaps be added that when civil affairs alone were in mind the expression used was *quoad civilia*. Although the distinction has now little significance, the terms are still used to denote two types of former

Church of Scotland charges, the *quoad omnia* parishes being quite simply those created prior to 1844. (To be strictly accurate, one should qualify that statement by saying that there were nine created in the course of the following twenty years.)

Heritors   The heritors of a parish are the owners of heritable property (lands and the buildings thereon) within it. Time was when these heritors had a duty enforceable in law to erect and maintain a parish Church capable of seating two-thirds of the examinable persons (those not under twelve years of age) resident in the parish; to erect and maintain a manse with suitable offices and garden attached; to provide a glebe; and out of the fruits of the land to pay a stipend. Most of these obligations continued with only slight modifications until the passing of the Church of Scotland (Property and Endowments) Act of 1925, which was passed in anticipation of and to facilitate the Union of 1929. This Act brought about quite revolutionary changes. Church and manse were in effect handed over to the national church which had thereafter to assume responsibility for their maintenance. Most of the obligation in respect of stipend was either completely obliterated or provision was made for it to be redeemed by the payment of a capital sum. Today the only vestige of all these duties still surviving is that in some cases the assessment for stipend has not been redeemed and owners of heritable property may well have an annual sum to pay in respect of this. In all cases nowadays such sums are paid to the General Trustees and not to the minister of the parish. For all practical purposes heritors in the old sense of the word can be said to have disappeared.

Burgh Churches These were also a product of the Industrial Revolution, a responsibility being laid upon burghs to provide places of worship adequate to the needs of the people. In all, some forty-five Burgh Churches are still extant, most of them in the cities. Each of these, generally, has an independent constitution, but for our purposes here they may be regarded as essentially similar to parishes *quoad omnia.*

2. How it all came about

With that very inadequate word of explanation let us return to our historical survey:

Prior to the time when the secessions began to occur, the Church of Scotland was vastly different in its form of government at congregational level from what we know today. It had no machinery for the management of its temporal affairs for the very simple but sufficient reason that it had no temporal affairs to manage! The responsibility for providing and maintaining church and manse buildings lay squarely on the shoulders of the heritors, the stipend and the right to the glebe vested in the minister on his induction and were no concern of the congregation; indeed, the congregation was usually sternly discouraged from being

curious in regard to such affairs. Even the
provision of Communion elements could be
taken care of. The only money for which the
congregation had any responsibility was the
income from collections taken at the church
door (or, in some cases, at the kirkyard gate)
and these were for the poor of the parish.
When for the first time collections came to be
called for in aid of what we should now call
'schemes' these were also attended to by the
Kirk Session. That, historically, is why to this
day the care of the poor and collections for
schemes are (under all but the Free Church
constitution) the exclusive affair of the Kirk
Session.

When on the occurrence of the first secession
a group broke away from the parent church
they, quite naturally, followed the pattern they
had known, as far at least as this was possible.
To the Kirk Session of the new breakaway
group was given the same responsibilities as
had been theirs under the establishment. This
was all right so far as it went, but it did not go
far enough since there was no-one to corres-
pond to the heritors. A most serious lack this,
for it was from those heritors that there had
come the whole material provision for the
parish. So each of these splinter-congregations
got busy and prepared a document known as a
'Constitution' which did two things: first, it
made provision for the holding of the heritable
property of the congregation by trustees, and
made all kind of arrangement as to what was to
happen to the property in the event of further

division or secession; and secondly, it made
provision for the oversight of the temporal
affairs by a Committee of Management. In
most cases today it is the latter part of the
document alone which has survived and which
has, wrongly, arrogated to itself the title of 'the
Constitution'. Former U.P. congregations all
belong to this group.

As has been said, the Industrial Revolution
presented the Kirk in Scotland with a terrifying
challenge because of the massive increase of
population in general and because of the
dramatic change in the pattern of its distribution throughout the country. It was not long
before the idea had to be abandoned of
creating new parishes with heritors bound to
provide them with their material necessities.
First the Chapel of Ease, and latterly the parish
quoad sacra, was the answer which the parish
church provided. Before a new parish *quoad
sacra* could be 'erected' the Presbytery had to
be satisfied on a number of points: that there
was a minimum statutory endowment to meet
the stipend, that there were adequate buildings, that a satisfactory constitution had been
framed. These constitutions were not at first
identical, but quickly they came to conform to a
common pattern. In particular, there began to
emerge a body whose name might vary quite a
bit but whose character remained fairly con-
stant and which had the responsibility for
looking after the temporal affairs. The Congregational Board was already in the making.

By the time the Free Church came into being

in 1843 this general pattern was becoming established, so they had a model on which to base their actions. The peculiar contribution of the Church of the Disruption, however, was the conception of the Deacons' Court. The use of the term 'deacon' was inspired, clearly, by the incident in *Acts* where deacons were appointed to relieve the apostles from the necessity of 'waiting on tables'. The odd thing was that the Free Church saw the Deacons' Court consisting not only of those chosen specifically to 'wait on tables' but also of the elders who on the strength of the New Testament precedent might have been expected to be relieved of this. The specialty of the Free Church principle was that the deacon was ordained and served on the Court for life. When in later years Free Church congregations increasingly adopted the idea of a limited period of office without ordination the whole system came to be almost identical with that of the Congregational Board.

Meanwhile in the old *quoad omnia* parishes the heritors were steadily divesting themselves of their responsibilities, and in the absence of any other body to take over these matters they fell to the lot of the Kirk Session. It is not strictly true to say, as is often done, that the traditional pattern in Scotland was that the Kirk Session looked after all the affairs of the congregation, spiritual and temporal. Traditionally, the eldership was recognised as exclusively a spiritual function, and it was only through force of circumstances that in those old parishes where there was no-one else available to do so the Kirk Session found itself loaded with temporal as well as spiritual functions.

The situation today, then, is that we have these four methods for dealing with temporal affairs:

First, in a decreasing number of *quoad omnia* parishes there is the Kirk Session in sole command.

Secondly, in former *quoad sacra* parishes, in cases of unions where differing traditions have been brought together, in newly created parishes, and in a considerable number of cases where a voluntary change to this system has been agreed by the congregation, the temporal affairs are in the hands of a Congregational Board consisting of the Elders along with a number of Elected Members from the congregation.

Thirdly, in former Free Church congregations there is likely to be a Deacons' Court made up of all the Elders and a comparable number of Deacons either ordained for life or elected for a period of years.

Fourthly, in former U.P. congregations there will usually be a Committee of Management differentiated from the two foregoing principally by the fact that it has probably no connection whatever with the Kirk Session, that it is most unlikely to include either Minister or Elders in its membership, and that it is very much more under the direction and control of the congregation in the discharge of its duties.

3. The Kirk Session

Procedure In those former *quoad omnia* charges which have not agreed to adopt the Model Constitution, the temporal affairs as well as the spiritual affairs of the congregation are under the direction and control of the Kirk Session, and the procedures followed by that court are the same no matter with which type of business it is dealing.

Property Although all, or nearly all, of the heritable property of such a charge is nowadays vested in the General Trustees it is most important to note: (*a*) the responsibility for its maintenance and for its being adequately insured lies with the Kirk Session; (*b*) no extraordinary repairs and no alterations, improvements or additions are to be made to any of the buildings without the prior consent both of the Presbytery and of the General Trustees; (*c*) no part of the property can be sold, let, or otherwise disposed of, nor can it be advanced in security for debt, without similar consent; and that indeed the Kirk Session has no power to grant any kind of disposition or lease of the property. While, of course, informal discussion with a potential purchaser or lessee may most helpfully be conducted at local level it is essential that the Presbytery and the Trustees be brought in before the stage of missives is reached.

Congregational Meeting An interesting situation arises when, as sometimes happens in a former *quoad omnia* parish, an annual congregational meeting is held to receive reports on the year's work, to approve accounts, etc. The rather anomalous position is that the Kirk Session is not answerable to the congregation and certainly should not be taking instructions from it; and yet unless they are to be free to offer criticisms and to pass resolutions the congregation can scarcely be expected to show much enthusiasm for attending such a meeting. One obvious way out of the dilemma is not to hold such a meeting at all, and there is certainly no obligation to do so. On the other hand there is much to be said for trying to spread interest in the work of the congregation by bringing the faithful together and discussing with them what is being done in their name, and with their contributions. After all, the modern congregation holds the ultimate sanction of withdrawing their financial support if things do not please them; and not all the constitutional autonomy of the Kirk Session will pay the bills! The idea is to ensure that any suggestions come in the form of recommendations and not of injunctions, and that when any changes are subsequently made these are effected in consequence of a decision of Kirk Session and not as the direct result of a congregational vote.

All the material already discussed in the chapter referring to Kirk Session business applies with equal force in the field of temporal affairs, as does what is said in the section on the Congregational Board on the matter of stipend (p. 53).

4. The Congregational Board

As has been indicated, the Congregational Board had its origin in the former *quoad sacra* congregation, but it is now the standard type of constitution and the church is committed to the policy of making it universal. As such it is conferred upon Church Extension charges when they achieve full status, and it is given to united congregations whose constituents had been operating different constitutions. In 1965 an *Amended Model Deed of Constitution for Parishes* Quoad Sacra was approved by the General Assembly. The same Assembly 're-commended and urged' congregations which had not already done so to adopt this model deed. Approximately seventy per cent of all congregations now operate under this method.

Who Are on the Board?

The Congregational Board consists of minister, elders, and a number of members elected by the congregation at its Stated Annual Meeting.

Minister The Moderator of Session, whether he be the minister or the interim moderator, is automatically a member of the Board.

Elders Normally all the elders are members of the Board in virtue of being members of the

Kirk Session. Provision is made, however, whereby the congregation may resolve to have the number reduced to an agreed figure which shall not be less than five for a congregation of under 200, eight when between 200 and 400, and twelve when over 400. Notice of such a proposal to reduce the representation of elders, along with an indication of the number to be substituted, must be given in the intimation calling the congregational meeting, and the motion must be carried by a majority of at least two-thirds of those present (not necessarily those voting). With the same reservation in regard to notice and to majority, such a resolution may at any time be rescinded so that all members of Session are once again members of the Board. In a case where it has been resolved to restrict the numbers, it is for the Kirk Session itself to decide how those elders will be chosen, who are to serve on the Board, and for how long they are to do so.

Elected Members These are appointed to the Board at the Stated Annual Meeting of the congregation. They are elected from the ranks of the congregation, being men or women of eighteen years of age or over. They must be members in the full sense; adherents are not eligible. The Model Deed does not itself provide a title for such persons and for want of a better I refer to them as 'Elected Members'. Their election is for a period of three years, at the end of which they are eligible for re-election. The number to be elected may be equal to, but must not exceed, the number of elders. This numerical superiority of the elders may be upset in the course of the year by death, removal, etc., but this does not seem to me to matter so long as at the time of the election the elders are in a majority. In the event of a decision being reached to reduce the number of elders, with a consequent need to 'lose' some of the elected members, it shall be for those members themselves to determine how their number is to be reduced to conform to that of the elders. In the event of the death, disqualification or resignation of one of the elected members the Board itself may appoint a duly qualified person to complete his term, subject to confirmation at the next Stated Annual Meeting.

Provision is made whereby the Presbytery may intervene in a case where a Board persists in disregarding the terms of the constitution 'after their attention has been called to the matter'. While the point is not beyond doubt in terms of the Act I take this to mean that the attention of the Board has been drawn to the irregularity in some official way by the Presbytery and not just that somebody in the congregation has written a letter about it. In such circumstances the Presbytery may remove from the Board those deemed guilty of such contumacy, declaring them ineligible for re-election for a period of three years. The Presbytery may then take what steps it thinks proper to fill the resulting vacancies. The Act does not make clear what effect such suspension will have upon the position of an elder or elders who have been declared guilty of this kind of contumacy, whether though suspended from the Board they continue to function on the Kirk Session. It is presumed it will be for the Presbytery to decide in any particular case what degree and sort of disciplinary action is appropriate.

It is worth noting that what was principally in the mind of those who drafted the Model Deed, when they made provision for a possible reduction in the number of elders, was the position of those congregations which have unusually large Kirk Sessions. In such cases under the old regulations either an equal number of elected members was appointed and a quite inordinately large and unwieldy Board resulted (a hundred and fifty and more was not uncommon) or else a disproportionately small number of elected members was added (say fifteen against eighty elders) thus putting the Kirk Session virtually in control of the Board. In all cases where the Kirk Session numbers more than, say, twenty-five it is suggested that serious consideration might be given to the advisability of working with a numerically reduced Board in this fashion. It will generally be found that there are elders keen to continue on the Session but perfectly happy to be relieved of the obligations which membership of the Board imposes.

Who Are the Officials of the Board?

Chairman The minister (or interim moderator in a vacancy) has the right *ex officio* to be

Chairman of the Board. He may, if he so desire, waive this right, and if he does so the Board (not the minister) appoints one of its number to act as its Chairman. My personal impression is that the minister who had relinquished the Chair would not be entitled (and I am quite sure he would not be wise) to reclaim, as it were, the right to the Chair at any time in the course of the year. Certainly he could do so when the Board was reconstituted after the next Stated Annual Meeting. And clearly if a new minister is inducted he is to be presumed to wish to accept the Chair whatever may have been the position in the days of his predecessor. It should be noted that the Act makes no provision for the appointment of a permanent Vice-Chairman. In the absence of the Chairman from a particular meeting those present elect one of their number to act *pro tempore*. And if they happen always to elect the same person that is their affair!

It is perhaps worthy of note that no matter who fills the post he is 'Chairman' and not 'Moderator' — the latter term should be reserved for the courts of the church. He has a casting vote only.

Clerk   At their first meeting after being elected the Board have to appoint a clerk (who need not necessarily be one of their own number). The clerk has to keep minutes of all meetings of the Board as well as of the Stated Annual Meeting and of any other congregational meetings held for temporal purposes.

Treasurer   The Board have also to appoint a

treasurer (who may be the same person as the clerk) to look after their finances. It is his duty to keep a separate banking account in name of the Board. In this connection an arrangement should be made whereby cheques drawn on this account require the signature of another person besides the treasurer. For convenience it is wise to nominate two or more such persons any one of whom may countersign the treasurer's cheques. It cannot be too strongly emphasised that the practice of such persons signing blank cheques in advance 'to save bother' defeats the whole purpose of the scheme. People should not be needlessly put in the way of temptation, and to say this is no slur upon their character.

Auditor It is for the Board annually to appoint, not necessarily from their own number though he may be, an auditor or auditors to examine the books and accounts of the treasurer. There is nothing to prevent the engagement of professional auditors and such a practice has advantages that go far to compensate for the expense involved.

How Does the Board Meet?

The constitutional position is that the Board meets when called by its Chairman, either by pulpit intimation or by personal notice. The Chairman must call a meeting within ten days if a quorum (see below) request him to do so. Within a month of the Stated Annual Meeting at which the new Board was elected a first meeting must, in terms of the Act, be called.

What actually happens in most cases is that Boards have an arrangement for regular monthly or similar meetings. Reference should be made to the chapter on the Kirk Session for suggestions in regard to agenda, opening and closing, approving minutes, etc. (pp. 15–17).

Quorum   When the Board numbers fewer than nine the quorum is three; when it numbers between nine and twenty the quorum is five; and for more than twenty it is seven.

What Does the Board Do?

The Board has the responsibility of seeing to the ingathering of all funds due to the congregation (apart from the Poor Fund and any other fund specifically under control of the Kirk Session). These include ordinary and special collections, seat rents (if any), special donations, income from endowments for congregational purposes, repayment of tax on Bonds of Annuity. Out of these revenues the Board has to meet (1) the payment of the stipend and the listed and travelling expenses of the minister; (2) the payment due to the Aged and Infirm Ministers' Fund based on a percentage of stipend; (3) expenses incurred in connection with the maintenance of public worship and the dispensing of the sacraments, including the cost of heating, lighting, and cleaning of the church and halls, rates, taxes and insurance, and salaries of organist and church officer; (4) expenses of maintenance of the manse; (5) Mission and Service Fund allocation; (6) General Assembly, Synod, and

Presbytery dues; (7) amount transferred to the Fabric Fund Account.

The Board has a duty not only to ingather funds and pay accounts but also to take all appropriate steps to see that the sums ingathered are adequate to meet the various commitments of the congregation. Primarily, however, the duty of impressing the congregation with a proper sense of stewardship lies with the Kirk Session, the duty of the Board being to ensure that the funds actually made available are dealt with in an orderly and responsible fashion.

Stipend   The stipend, listed expenses, and travelling expenses are all as these have been agreed with the Presbytery and concurred in by the Assembly's Committee on the Maintenance of the Ministry in a Vacancy Schedule (see p. 56). Endowments for stipend are paid directly to the minister and the congregational contribution towards stipend has, since 1975, been transmitted by Banker's Order to the office of the Maintenance of the Ministry Committee which is then directly responsible for the payment of all stipends and which remits the appropriate monthly sums to the ministers' banking accounts. The Model Deed, however, requires that at some point in the congregational accounts there should be shown the amount actually received by the minister by way of stipend in respect of the year in question.

Fabric   In regard to property the Board has the responsibility of seeing that this is properly maintained in a sound condition and that it is adequately covered by insurance. For the former purpose a Fabric Fund should be maintained out of which all (and not just extraordinary) expenditure on maintenance and repairs should be met. A fixed sum should be transferred each year from the Ordinary Revenue Fund to this account. This transfer should be made each year irrespective of how much has actually been spent on fabric in that year — who knows when an extraordinarily heavy account will be incurred calling for all the reserves available.

Too much cannot be made of the fact that while fabric is the easiest thing on which to save money (re-slating can always be put off for another year) it is by far the most dangerous. What a few pounds could put right today may cost hundreds next year and thousands in a couple of years' time.

Extraordinary repairs to fabric or additions or alterations to property should not in the normal way be charged to the Fabric Fund but should be the subject of a special and specific effort. Work on such a project should not be put in hand without consent of the Presbytery (and of the General Trustees when the property is vested in them) or before funds are in hand or detailed arrangements for their ingathering have been approved.

Property Register   The Board has a duty to appoint from its membership or by co-option a Fabric Committee including at least one person with technical knowledge and experience, and that Committee shall generally watch over the property. In particular it shall at least once a year conduct a thorough inspection of all property belonging to or held for behoof of the congregation. Such a body is entitled to require admittance to the Manse. It shall also keep a Property Register in which shall be set forth full particulars regarding the property, including information about title-deeds etc., as well as a record of work carried out upon it in the course of each year, and a note of the amount of the insurance cover. This Register is to be submitted annually to the Presbytery at the time of the visitation of records.

Stated Annual Meeting   A date not later than 31st March is to be fixed by the Board when, after two Sundays' intimation, the Stated Annual Meeting of the congregation is to be held at which elections shall be made to the Board and at which also the Treasurer shall submit the duly audited Statement of Accounts made up as at 31st December or such earlier date as has been agreed. The Presbytery may authorise in any year a later date being fixed for the meeting on adequate cause shown; but if the meeting is not held before 31st March without permission for delay having been obtained it is for the Kirk Session to report the situation to the Presbytery which will then take appropriate action. The meeting will normally be held in the church or church hall but may be held in some other place (a village hall, for example) so long as clear indication of the meeting-place is given in the notice.

Credit Balance In the event that there is a credit balance remaining in the Revenue and Expenditure Account after the various commitments have been fully met, this may be applied to any or all of the following purposes: (*a*) supplement to stipend; (*b*) additional transfer to Fabric Fund Account; (*c*) extra payment to Mission and Service Fund Account or to any specific object within that; (*d*) payment to a General Reserve or Contingency Account; or (*e*) the creation of a Special Reserve Account. Any supplement to stipend that will have the effect of increasing it beyond the appropriate figure shall be made only with permission of Presbytery, which may require additions to be made also to the amount of Aid Given and to the amount of the Mission and Service Fund contribution. The use made of any balance as above shall be included in the report given to the congregation at the Stated Annual Meeting.

Stipend Arrangements When a vacancy has occurred in a congregation and permission has been given to call a minister, immediately a Vacancy Schedule is issued to the Congregational Treasurer, and it is for the Board in conference with the Presbytery's Maintenance of the Ministry Committee to complete this, showing fully the arrangements proposed in respect of Stipend, Listed Expenses, Aid to be given to or to be drawn from the Minimum Stipend Fund. It is a first duty of the Board thereafter to ensure that the obligations undertaken in this Schedule are honoured in full.

Should changing circumstances render impossible the fulfilment of these obligations a Revision Schedule may be asked for, and if this is granted revised terms may be agreed which will thereafter form the basis for the payment of stipend and in respect of aid whether given or received.

Supplement to Pension   Occasionally when a minister retires there is a desire within the Board to recognise his services to the congregation by undertaking an annual payment in supplement of his annuity from the Aged and Infirm Ministers' Fund. Clearly it is important that this should not be done at the expense of his successor, which is the inevitable result of blithely agreeing to the payment of an annual allowance. Regulations approved by the General Assembly of 1976 provide that such augmentation shall be paid only by a self-supporting congregation which has met in full its obligations in respect of Stipend, Aid, and Mission and Service, and that it shall consist in the provision of a capital sum for the purchase of an annuity to be payable to the retired minister.

5. The Deacons' Court

The Deacons' Court has its origin in the former Free Church, having taken shape in terms of Acts of Assembly of that body of 1846 and 1847. In essence it has today points of marked similarity with the Congregational Board. Its original design, however, was based upon the principle that however much the duties of deacons and elders might differ the character of their appointment was identical.

The deacon, having been elected by the congregation, was ordained by the Kirk Session and held office for life.

Who Are On the Court?

Minister   The minister is *ex officio* a member of the Court and in the case of a vacant congregation the interim moderator takes the place of the minister on the Court.

Elders   The elders are all *ex officio* members of the Deacons' Court. It is said that 'the higher office Scripturally includes the lower' and that accordingly the elders 'are not excluded from the exercise of the Deacons' function'.

Deacons   These are men or women over eighteen years of age, in full communion with the congregation, who have been elected to office by the congregation at the annual meeting or at a meeting specially called for the purpose. It is the Kirk Session which determines when an election of deacons is to be held and how many deacons are to be appointed, but it is only the congregation which can elect them. The method of election is as in the case of elders (p. 4). It is recommended that elections to Session and to Court should not be made at the same meeting.

The original practice was that deacons, having been elected, were ordained to office by the Kirk Session (in face of the congregation) and that they continued in office until death, resignation, or disqualification. If a deacon is absent from meetings for a year without adequate cause known, the Kirk Session (not the Deacons' Court) may, after giving him due notice, declare that he has ceased to be a member of the Deacons' Court.

The pattern that is more generally found today, however, is that deacons are appointed to office for a period of three years. They are not ordained, but, instead, on the first convenient Sunday after their election their names are read out at church service and they are commended to God in prayer.

A congregation may at any time resolve to change from the older to the newer method, and such a decision is to be taken at a congregational meeting called on the authority of the Kirk Session for that express purpose after two Sundays' notice. The decision may be reached either by open vote or by the use of ballot papers. When a resolution to change has been approved then either those deacons who have been ordained may elect to retain that status (in which case they will remain on the Court without their names being at any time submitted for re-election) or they may decide to relinquish their life-status and submit themselves for re-election in the usual way. When a union of congregations has been effected on the understanding that the united congregation will adopt the Model Constitution then if one of the uniting congregations had deacons ordained for life they may likewise elect to be life-long members of the Congregational

Board or they may relinquish that right and become elected members in the ordinary fashion.

Who Are Officials of the Court?

Chairman The minister or interim moderator presides over the Deacons' Court. In his absence the Court chooses one of its number to act *pro tempore*. The Chairman (who sits as Chairman and not as Moderator) has a casting vote only. He cannot move a resolution but he can introduce business and may address the Court upon it.

Clerk The Court is required to appoint a Clerk who shall keep a record of its proceedings. In his absence a Clerk *pro tempore* should be appointed. In either case the oath *de fideli* should be administered on appointment.

Treasurer The Court also appoints a Treasurer who is responsible for all congregational funds including the Poor Fund but excepting those specifically entrusted to the Kirk Session.

Officer The Church Officer has, as one of his duties, that of being Officer of the Deacons' Court and of being in attendance, when required, at its meetings.

How Does the Court Meet?

The convening of the Deacons' Court is the responsibility of the minister but with this specialty, that in a time of vacancy it is for the Clerk and not for the interim moderator to call meetings. Meetings are normally called by pulpit intimation but they may be called by notice sent to each member. It is normal for meetings to be held monthly and indeed in the original legislation this was set down as a minimum. Any three members may requisition a meeting. The requisition is to be addressed to the Chairman and although there is no requirement to this effect I should certainly think the requisition should be in writing. Meetings are normally in private (because, I imagine, of the involvement with the Poor Fund) but exception may be made if desired. The Deacons' Court cannot meet when the Kirk Session is sitting, nor, except with special permission, at the time of a meeting of any of the superior courts. For particulars about minutes, etc., see the chapter on the Kirk Session (p. 16).

Quorum No matter what the size of the Court, three forms a quorum and it is not necessary, as with the Session, that one of these should be the minister.

What Does the Court Do?

The limitations of the powers of the Deacons' Court are clearly set forth in the original Free Church Act — 'The Deacons' Court has no power of discipline over its own members. It can neither admit to the office of Deaconship not depose from it. Nor can the resignation of a Deacon be competently received by the Deacons' Court nor dealt with by them in any way. But the Deacons' Court is entitled to certified extracts from the minutes of Kirk Session insofar as by admission,

removal, suspension, or deposition of office-
bearers these minutes affect its membership;
and any change of which the Court thus
obtains evidence ought to be recorded.' It
will have been noted above that it is the Kirk
Session which takes action against the absentee
deacon. It should be particularly noted that
it is only the Kirk Session that can deal with
a deacon's resignation from office.

The Deacons' Court has the management
and charge of the whole property, heritable
and moveable, of the congregation and is
required to apply spiritual principles in the
conduct of these temporal affairs.

Church Buildings It should be explained
that Free Church property is normally held in
name of a small number of office-holders in
virtue of their office and that the titles include
provision (the 'Free Church clauses') whereby
the property cannot be disposed without the
authority of the General Assembly.

It is for the Deacons' Court to ensure that the
place of worship, the halls, the manse, and
other property held for the congregation are
maintained in a proper state of repair, and it is
for them too to take steps to raise whatever
funds are necessary for this purpose. Building
operations or repairs, however, must not be
put in hand without the prior sanction of the
Presbytery. An Act of 1932 determines the
rather delicate relationship between the minister and the Court in regard to the use of the
church property. The Deacons' Court cannot
grant the use of any of the church buildings for

any purpose whatever without the consent of
the minister. It cannot withhold the use of the
buildings for any congregational purpose or
for a meeting of a religious, ecclesiastical or
charitable nature which has the blessing of the
minister. But no meeting for any other purpose can be held in the buildings, with or
without the minister's approval, unless the
Deacons' Court has acquiesced. This is today
accepted as the general rule throughout the
church in regard to granting the use of church
property.

Servants The Kirk Session appoints the
Church Officer, but the Deacons' Court fixes
(as well as pays) his salary. In the case of
doorkeepers and others employed in connection with the convenience of worshippers the
Deacons' Court has power to engage, dismiss,
and to fix terms of service as well as to pay. The
organist is appointed by the Kirk Session which
may confer, if so advised, with the Deacons'
Court before making an appointment. Subject
to the same qualification about conferring the
fixing of the terms of service of the organist is
Session business, the fixing of his salary is
Deacons' Court business.

Funds There is a specialty in the case of the
Deacons' Court in that it and not the Kirk
Session is responsible for the care of poor
persons connected with the congregation. For
this purpose it may appoint special collections
or use other means for raising funds. In olden
days the Deacons' Court had a particular
responsibility in connection with the Sustenta-

tion Fund (Maintenance of the Ministry) and it was common practice for the deacons to share with the elders the care of a district and to visit therein in pursuit of these financial matters. Today the arrangements for stipend are as in *quoad sacra* charges and reference should be made to page 56.

Congregational Meeting   It is for the Court, as soon as the year's accounts have been audited, to call a meeting of the congregation at which these may be submitted for approval. At this meeting suggestions may be offered by members of the congregation in regard to future distribution of funds, these being merely suggestions for the consideration of the Court.

Auditors   At the annual meeting two members of the congregation are appointed to act as auditors for the following year.

6. The Committee of Management

Each congregation of the former United Presbyterian Church had its own individual constitution. This, as has been explained above, properly consisted of two separate and distinct parts, the first a set of provisions as to how the heritable property was to be held, and the second 'Rules for the Administration of the Temporal Affairs of the Congregation'. It is this latter section which today is usually referred to as 'the constitution', which is misleading. Power is given in the constitution itself for its terms to be altered, but only after a proposal to this effect has been 'entertained' at one congregational meeting and approved at the next, and then only with concurrence of the Presbytery. Advantage has, naturally, been taken of this provision and congregations have effected various and varied changes, so that although all congregational constitutions began, probably, by adhering fairly closely to the Model set forth in the Handbook they nowadays vary quite considerably in detail. It is not always easy to lay hands on a reliable up-to-date copy of what are the terms of the local constitution.

An Act of 1970 requires that wherever this system is operated, a copy of the document applying within that particular congregation is to be supplied to any candidate immediately on his nomination in the vacancy. Since, as will be pointed out hereunder, the minister has no status on the Committee of Management, the purpose of this Act is to ensure that before accepting nomination he will know clearly just how the congregation's temporal affairs are administered.

Who Are the Managers?

The Committee of Management consists of a definite number determined by the congregation itself, of Managers, being members in full communion with the congregation, elected by the congregation, normally at its annual meeting (though in some cases the election may be by voting papers completed and returned in advance of the meeting). Women may be

elected only if a resolution to that effect has
been approved at a congregational meeting
called for the purpose. I am not aware that in
any of the constitutions it is specifically laid
down that the ministers and elders are not
eligible for election like other members of the
congregation, but in very few cases is the
minister in fact regarded as eligible, and there
are many cases where a well-established tradition prevails that a person cannot simultaneously be an elder and a manager; appointment
to one office automatically involves resignation
from the other.

In the case of a manager who has died,
removed, or been suspended from office (or
from membership of the congregation) an
appointment may be made to fill the vacancy,
this being done not by the managers but by the
congregation at a meeting specially called for
the purpose. A person so elected completes the
unfinished period of service of the manager he
replaces. One-third of the managers retire
annually and are normally eligible for re-
election. Elections are held on the occasion of
the annual congregational meeting.

As with deacons, it is recommended that on
the first convenient Sunday after election the
minister during service should read over the
names of those elected and commend them to
God in prayer.

Who Are Officials of the Managers?

Preses In some cases the congregation itself
elects, in others it empowers the Committee to

elect, one of the managers to act as Preses. It should be noted that he is 'Preses of the Managers' and not, as is sometimes suggested, 'Preses of the Congregation'. He carries all the normal responsibilities of a chairman — to see the meetings are opened and closed with prayer, to ensure that that fact is minuted, to see that the business is orderly conducted and properly recorded. He has a deliberative as well as a casting vote and may introduce business and speak upon it. He takes the chair at the Annual Business Meeting and at any special meetings called for temporal purposes. The general tradition is that the minister is expected to attend at the opening of such a meeting and to constitute it with prayer, after which he is encouraged to depart. In the absence of the Preses from a meeting of the Committee of Management the managers elect one of their number to preside.

Clerk The congregation also either itself elects, or empowers the committee to elect from their number, a clerk who is to keep a minute-book recording the doings of the committee and also of congregational meetings for temporal purposes and to make this accessible to managers at all reasonable times.

Treasurer Likewise a treasurer is appointed either by the congregation or by the managers and he carries through all the normal duties of such an office.

Auditors Two members of the congregation, not themselves managers, are appointed at the annual meeting to act as auditors of the

treasurer's books for the coming year and to
report at next annual meeting.

How Do the Managers Meet?

Regular meetings are held at least quarterly.
They are called by the preses, or in his absence
by the clerk, by pulpit intimation or by personal
notice. One-third of the managers can requisition the calling of a meeting. The quorum is
three, or one-third of the total number when
there are more than nine.

The rules for the conduct of business etc are
as for the Kirk Session (p. 16).

What Do the Managers Do?

The Committee of Management is generally
very jealous of its powers and it is important
therefore to note that these powers are strictly
limited, on the one side by reference to the
congregation and on the other by reference
to the Session. The Constitution itself sets
quite specific limits to, for example, the
amount which the managers may spend on
repairs without reference to a special congregational meeting, and also expressly forbids
them to burden the property with debt without
similar special authority. And every U.P. constitution has a clause in these or similar terms:
'The constitutional right of the Kirk Session to
watch over all the interests of the congregation,
and to interpose whenever, in its opinion, the
welfare of the congregation calls on it to do so,
by convening meetings for any purpose connected with congregational matters, or in any

other competent manner, is expressly reserved.'

I remember a case where a Kirk Session had
intervened in this way to the annoyance of the
managers, one of whom gave notice of his
intention at the next annual meeting to propose the deletion from the constitution of the
whole of the offending paragraph. He did not
take kindly to my pointing out that this section
merely declared the law and did not create it,
and that the removal of the section even if it
were competent, would not alter the position in
the slightest. In passing, attention may be
drawn to the rather anomalous statement that
nothing in this 'constitution' is to affect the
'constitutional right' of the Kirk Session, etc.,
which seems to support my criticism of the use
of the word 'constitution' to describe what are
truly the rules for the administration of the
temporal affairs of the congregation. It is not
without interest to note, too, how the term
'competent manner' contrives to beg the question.

It is also expressly affirmed that the managers have no jurisdiction over the conduct of
public worship, and that while they are required to apply spiritual principles to the
management of temporal affairs they have no
degree of spiritual rule and no authority to
review the actions of minister or Kirk Session.

Within these limitations the Committee of
Management have very wide jurisdiction in the
running of the temporal affairs of the congregation. The Church Officer is appointed

and dismissed by Kirk Session and managers jointly, meetings in this connection being presided over by the Moderator of Session and recorded in the Session minutes. Doorkeepers and other subordinate officials are appointed by the managers. They have the same restrictions over their power in respect of buildings as apply in the case of the Deacons' Court (p. 62). Special meetings of the congregation for temporal purposes are called by authority of the managers and presided over by the preses, but the agreement of the Session has first of all to be obtained before such a meeting can be called.

In some constitutions provision is made whereby the stipend is to be fixed by the congregation at the annual meeting. This I take to be superseded by the general regulations approved by the General Assembly in regard to stipend being determined by the Presbytery in conjunction with the Assembly's Committee on the Maintenance of the Ministry. An increase beyond the Appropriate in any one year might still be resolved upon by the congregation, but even that would be subject to approval at Presbytery level. (For regulations governing stipend generally see p. 56).

7. Changing the Method

In the early '60's a special committee of Assembly gave consideration to the difficulties created in the church in consequence of the diversity in method of administration of temporal affairs as between one congregation and its neighbour. As a result of the labours of this body changes were made in the character of the Congregational Board to meet criticisms that had been levelled against it. For it was clearly the opinion of the Committee that this was the method to be commended for universal adoption.

The principle of management by the Kirk Session alone, held by many (particularly ministers) to be the ideal method was felt to be quite undemocratic and to suffer through its failure to involve the rank and file of the membership at the level of decision-making. In the old days when the provision for temporal needs came from outwith the congregation and was guaranteed by law such a system could be justified, but today when the congregation can manifest their disapproval by withholding their financial support and so in effect negate an unpopular Kirk Session decision it is reasonable, surely, to seek their co-operation all along the line.

The former U.P. method at the opposite extreme has proved enormously effective in many cases and there are not wanting ministers who welcome a situation where they are not constantly beset by financial worries. But the system suffers from a tendency towards an absolute separation of the financial from the spiritual, and however neat this may be in a theoretical way it is no reflection of reality. For there to be one body with, for example, absolute power to decide to hold a week-night service while a totally separate body has equally absolute authority to say they can't afford the cost of heating the church that night — surely there are unhappy possibilities here.

The Deacons' Court, on the other hand, by tending, as it has been doing, to drop the 'for-life' principle in favour of appointment for a three-year period has in fact been more and more approximating to identity with the Model Deed type of Congregational Board.

The Committee, however, did not suggest that the Assembly should go further than to 'recommend and urge' the adoption of the Model Deed. To render this more attractive the method for making a change was considerably simplified.

When a Kirk Session considers it is wise to think about making a change in the method of managing temporal affairs it summons a congregational meeting on two Sundays' notice. If the congregation approves, then the matter is reported to the Presbytery which, having concurred, informs the Delegation of Assembly, and the official Deed of Constitution is issued. In the case where a former U.F. congregation elects to adopt the Model Deed it is under no obligation (as once it was) to transfer its property into name of the General Trustees though, of course, it is always at liberty to do so.

When two congregations are united it is usual to write into the Basis of Union that the temporal affairs shall be administered according to the Model Deed and this ensures that the Delegation of Assembly will, without the need for any further meetings at local level, issue such a Deed once the union has been effected. If, however, the two congregations had operated under the same constitution (other than the Model one) it is in order for the united congregation to decide to continue under that same constitution.

3

Coping with a Vacancy

For close on a hundred and fifty years, between the early-18th and the mid-19th centuries, the Kirk in Scotland was torn asunder over the principle of patronage: the right (restored in 1712) by which the chief heritor within a parish made the presentation of the 'living' of that parish to a minister of his own choosing. At its worst the system was probably responsible for as few serious misfits in parishes as any subsequent system of popular election has been, and its operation was kept within bounds by the fact that the Presbytery had not only the right to induct but also, before induction, to take the presentee on trials and satisfy itself that he was qualified for the appointment. Scotland never suffered, as did her southern neighbour, from the presentation of livings to men who had no standing as ministers but who were free to employ vicars to act in their stead and pay them a pittance for the income of the parish.

The rising tide of democratic consciousness demanded, however, that a minister's acceptability to the congregation was every bit as relevant and far more important as a qualification than was his knowledge of Greek or Hebrew. So we had the secessions one after another from 1733 and finally, in 1843, we had the Disruption. Or perhaps it would be more correct to say that the end of the story was reached in 1874 with the abolition for good and all of patronage within the Kirk.

It is not surprising, then, that the right to call a minister of its own choosing should be so dearly treasured by our congregations. It is inevitable too that a right which people were determined should not be infringed should be hedged about with complicated restrictions and should be operated under elaborate regulations. Sometimes, particularly when they are in a hurry and the regulations get in their way, people talk exasperatedly about them as 'red tape' and want to see them cut out. I have on occasion been tempted to reply, 'Red tape, yes, because it is stained with the blood of your fathers.'

It is this red tape that I should like to try to unravel, this complicated legislation that I should like to try to explain, in this chapter.

However, before the vacancy machinery can be set in motion today it is necessary for a vacant congregation to be granted permission to call, and even when permission has been so given there are occasionally restrictions imposed upon the field of choice open to the congregation. That is to say, the first step in any vacancy is to have the question of possible readjustment duly disposed of. And this is a large field and one whose exploration can occupy a lot of time.

What I have to say, then, will be divided into two sections: first, the readjustment procedure; and secondly, the vacancy procedure. But first one or two general points.

1. What is a Vacancy?

Let us begin by clarifying what we mean by our terms and ask first what is meant by a vacancy and how it is caused. A charge which has a minister inducted to it *ad vitam aut culpam*, or introduced to it on a terminable basis, is described during the continuance of the incumbency as 'full'. When the incumbency ends the church becomes 'vacant'. A vacancy may occur because the minister (*a*) has died, (*b*) has been translated and inducted to another parish, (*c*) has demitted the charge either in the ordinary way of retirement or to enable him to take up some other kind of appointment, or (*d*) has been deposed or deprived by the Presbytery. The date of the occurrence of any of these events is the date of the vacancy.

Ad Vitam aut Culpam

A word should be said in explanation of a phrase that will recur rather often: induction *ad vitam aut culpam*. In a day when stipend and other rights of the minister vested in him in virtue of his being minister it was important that he should be inducted, and such induction was always for life, or until some heinous moral fault had led to his deposition. This, under patronage, was a salutory provision ensuring that though the patron had the right to 'hire' he had no corresponding right to 'fire'. This position continued uninterrupted until 1972 when an Act of that year ordained that induction *ad vitam aut culpam* should cease and that on his attaining the age of seventy years a man's ministry should terminate as though he had demitted his charge on that date. (He might thereafter be continued on a *de die in diem* basis.) In spite of this Act it is still customary to speak of an unrestricted induction as being *ad vitam aut culpam*. Since no-one seems to have come up with a proper Latin tag, the simplest plan is to take it that the attainment of the age of seventy constitutes a fault culpable within the meaning of the Act!

Raising the Question

Immediately on the occurrence of a vacancy caused by death, or by anticipation in other cases, the Presbytery appoints an interim moderator to act in the vacancy and by his presence to enable the Kirk Session to function. Normally such an interim moderator has no standing whatever until the vacancy has actually occurred, but an Act of 1960 has provided that where an interim moderator has been appointed in a 'prospective vacancy' he may preside over meetings of Kirk Session concerned with matters connected with that vacancy (the moderator proper continuing to be responsible for all other ongoing business) and indeed with special permission of Presbytery procedure in the vacancy may be advanced as far as the appointment of the Vacancy Committee although the charge is still full.

The next step which the Presbytery has to take is that of expressing an 'opinion' on whether or not the question of readjustment should be raised. This 'opinion' is conveyed to the Assembly's Committee on Unions and Readjustments which in turn decides whether to share the opinion expressed or to disagree with it. An opinion that the question ought to be raised does not commit anyone to any specific position in regard to the shape of the future, it does not even necessarily imply that there is a *prima facie* case for readjustment. All it claims is that the matter is worth looking into. It is most unlikely that the Assembly's Committee will do other than concur in such an opinion and it is difficult to see how even the congregation concerned can seriously contest so modest an averment. Once the question has been raised the Presbytery orders that procedure in the vacancy shall be sisted until it has been settled.

At the same time that it concurs in the Presbytery's decision that the question should be raised, the Assembly's Committee always refers the case to the 'Synodical Conveners'. These are members of the Committee particularly responsible for the charges within a certain area. Their experience and expertise are always available to the Presbytery Sub-

Committee which is handling the case, and not infrequently when difficulties arise they are called in to lend weight to the local effort. The initiative, however, always lies at Presbytery level.

If the Presbytery's opinion is that the question of readjustment does not arise then that would seem to justify the granting to the congregation of permission to proceed with the calling of a minister without restriction. It would seem to me, however, that before such permission was given it would be important that the opinion should have crystallised into a 'decision' to the same effect, and this, I imagine, could occur only when the Assembly's Committee had indicated that it was of the same opinion.

It should be noted that the fact that it has been resolved to raise the question does not preclude a subsequent decision that the congregation should be allowed to call without restriction.

2. Readjustment Procedure

Let us suppose that a decision has been reached by Presbytery and concurred in by the Assembly's Committee that the question of readjustment is to be raised, what happens next?

In some cases the decision to raise the question will have been reached by the Presbytery without consultation with local parties; it was such an obvious case. In other instances a preliminary survey will have been carried out involving conference at local level. Certainly once the question has been raised a Committee will be appointed by Presbytery (most likely a sub-committee of its own Readjustments Committee) to meet with the local office-bearers and discuss the issue. Occasionally a Kirk Session insists that it alone should be involved in such debate, but usually all of the office-bearers are brought in which means, in effect, that the conferring body is the Congregational Board or the Deacons' Court or the elders and managers, as the case may be. In general terms it is desirable to have as wide a cross-section of congregational opinion represented as possible.

Why Readjustment?

There are today many factors contributing towards the necessity for looking very narrowly at every vacancy as it occurs with a view to assessing the possibilities for readjustment. For one thing there is the shortage of ministerial manpower with the consequent demand that the limited number of ministers available should be deployed to the best strategic advantage. For another thing there is the terrifying increase in the cost of the maintenance of buildings, with a need therefore to ensure that only those are retained which territorially are strictly necessary. There is the increasing cost of keeping a minister and the need to ensure that aid from the Maintenance of the Ministry is used only for essential charges. Yet again, there is the fact that our peculiar ecclesiastical history has led to considerable duplication (indeed triplication) of places of worship within the one area so that you have churches standing cheek-by-jowl. It is of supreme importance for a national church to secure that needy and deprived areas are not left churchless because of local financial stringency, but if this is to be achieved it can be only by preventing needless and meaningless duplication and overlapping in more prosperous areas.

Possibilities of the Situation

The object of the visiting committee will be, then, to discover how far the vacant congregation can contribute towards the solution of these problems by accepting some form of readjustment. Apart altogether from the willingness of the vacant congregation, the future pattern will to a considerable extent be determined by the situation in the area generally. For, as the law stands, the Presbytery can exert pressure only on the vacant congregation. If a congregation is 'full' it will be involved in readjustment only if the minister on the one hand and the congregation on the other are prepared to accept and concur in any proposals which the Presbytery may make. So that readjustment has of necessity to be an occasional and an opportunist exercise.

In a word, the visiting committee is not interested in a theoretical assessment of what would be the ideal church-pattern in the area but only in the very practical question of what form of readjustment can possibly be achieved given the situation as it actually exists. And these can produce two very different answers.

The probability is that after preliminary talks with the office-bearers of the vacant congregation the Committee will have to carry its investigation into other quarters. If some other congregation be found interested in the possibility of pursuing union or linking then normally each set of office-bearers appoints a limited number (say half-a-dozen) of their members to get together with the presbytery's committee and examine the possibilities more closely.

If it appears, either on the face of things or after due exploration, that there is no possibility of progress along the line of union or linking then the Committee may either conclude that the vacant congregation should be given permission to call or it should resume consideration of other possible forms of readjustment. What are the possibilities of readjustment?

3. Union

First of all there is the possibility of two or more congregations being united to become one congregation. This if agreed by the congregations concerned and by the Presbytery may be effected by the Presbytery with concurrence of the Assembly's Unions and Readjustments and Maintenance of the Ministry

Committees. There are a few cases, however, which have to go to the Assembly or their Commission.

Basis of Union The first step on the way towards effecting union is the preparation of a Basis of Union which provides for what will happen when union has been achieved: for the choice of a name for the congregation; for the property and funds becoming those of the united congregation; for the choice of a building as the place of worship and for the use or disposal of redundant property; for the merging of Kirk Sessions and Congregational Boards; for the delimitation of a parish area; for the choice of a manse and for the disposal of the redundant manse; and for the position in regard to a minister. It is the last of these which can lead to most complications.

Minister Retiring Where, as is commonly the case, one charge is full and the other is vacant it may be that the minister of the full charge is prepared to retire to facilitate the union. In such a case the Basis may allow him the use for life of the redundant manse, and if he is fairly near retiring age the Aged and Infirm Ministers' Fund will normally be prepared to accept him as an annuitant although before the regular time. The united congregation will thus be vacant and will be free to proceed to the election of a minister. (It is possible that even the united congregation so created is not thought deserving of a full ministry and if restrictions are to be imposed this will be made clear in the Basis of Union.)

Where a Vacancy Committee is being appointed after a union has been agreed it is wise that the two congregations should agree on an equitable division of the number each should appoint and that they should meet separately before union to appoint their respective shares. The alternative of waiting till the union has been effected and having the Vacancy Committee appointed at a meeting of the united congregation is not a satisfactory method.

Minister Retiring After a Period   It may be on the other hand that it has been acceptable to both sides that the 'sitting' minister should be first minister of the united congregation on the understanding that he will retire after a specified period. This can be a very satisfactory solution, providing, as it does, that there is on the spot over this difficult period not only a minister but a minister with unrivalled knowledge of the problems and personalities involved. In such a case the union will be effected as with a sitting minister and the vacancy when it occurs will proceed in the normal way. The minister will still be recognised as retiring in the interests of union although the date of his retirement does not coincide with the date of union.

I have always taken the view that when a Basis of Union provides for the retirement of a minister and has been accepted by him there is no need for the Presbytery to deal with his demission as it would in the case of a normal retirement. I think it is right, however, that at the first meeting after the union has taken place the minister (now retired) should be summoned to the presbytery and suitable notice should be taken of the fact of his retirement.

Minister Continuing Or it may be that union is to be effected under the minister of one of the charges. Such an arrangement can become effective only if both congregations approve and if the minister also approves; that is to say, not only the congregation being asked to accept the minister but also the congregation whose minister he is has the right to refuse, and if it does so the Presbytery cannot proceed. In a union of this kind it is usual for the Presbytery to meet at one of the churches for the purpose of declaring the congregations united and of introducing the minister as first minister of the united charge. The Act suggests there may be cases where 'induction' rather than 'introduction' is appropriate, but I cannot myself believe that in the present state of the law in regard to teinds, etc., induction can ever be a necessity.

Deferred Union A further complication emerges when the two congregations agree that they will unite but the vacant congregation insists it will enter into union only when the other congregation is vacant. This leads to what is called a Deferred Union. When agreement has been reached and approved on such a union the vacant congregation is allowed to call a minister who will in due course become minister of the united charge. To this end the congregation which is not immediately affected appoints members to act on a Joint Vacancy Committee, and in due course the person nominated has to be elected by that congregation as well as by the vacant one. Immediately the full charge becomes vacant the union becomes operative without further negotiation, and all that remains is for the Presbytery to arrange a service for the declaration of union and the introduction of the minister.

Should the minister so elected leave for any reason before a vacancy occurs in the other charge then the whole deferred union arrangement has to be regarded as frustrated and a fresh look taken at the situation as it then exists. The Act says that such a circumstance 'shall not prejudice an immediate union under the existing minister'. This can only mean that such a union is one of the possibilities of the case and cannot be taken to imply any commitment so to unite. Agreement to a second deferred union seems equally to be a possibility.

Preliminary Work The Basis of Union (whether immediate or deferred) confines itself very properly to general directions such as that the elders of the two Kirk Sessions shall form with the minister the Kirk Session of the united congregation. It makes no provision for such delicate matters as which of the Session Clerks shall be Clerk of the united Kirk Session, how the Woman's Guild branches will function after union, what will be the position of the Boys' Brigade officers, who will be organist: and so you can go on and draw up a list of quite terrifying choices. And, make no mistake, it is largely upon the degree of tact and wisdom and patience — and firmness — with which these questions are faced that the success or otherwise of the union will largely depend.

It is important, therefore, once the principle of union has been accepted, and certainly not later than when the Basis has been approved by both sides, that some kind of Steering Committee should be appointed to smooth the way for the merging of the two bodies. Under no circumstances should the union be allowed to occur before these issues have been fully explored. This is a field where the Presbytery can be of little avail and where everything depends upon local knowledge and initiative.

Freedom to Change Every Basis of Union has a clause at the end declaring that its terms are merely an instrument to allow a union to be effected and are not an excerpt from the laws of the Medes and the Persians, the united congregation being 'free like other congregations to adjust arrangements under authority of the Presbytery as need may arise'. Now suppose that two congregations neither of which was prepared to sacrifice its name agree to unite under the composite title of St David's in the Dumps and St Paul's in the Doldrums. It may well be that after a couple of years it is thought wise to change the name to, say, St Hubert's on the Heights. Then in my view they, like any other congregation, would simply apply to the Presbytery for permission to change and, the Presbytery concurring, the change would become effective.

It would not be necessary to obtain consent of the Assembly's Committee nor, even if that were possible, to change the Basis of Union. I raise this question of changing the Basis because to me it appears clear that once a Basis of Union has been employed to effect the union it becomes an historic document and you can no more change it than, halfway to Euston the Royal Scot could change its departure time from Central. If some change is proposed which appears to be to the prejudice of an interest deliberately protected in the Basis then I think the Presbytery decision might well be expressed as, 'Notwithstanding the terms of Clause X of the Basis of Union it was agreed that. . . .' But I am sure it would not be necessary to have the concurrence of all who had approved the Basis in the first place.

4. Linking

The linking of two (or more) congregations means quite simply that while retaining their separate identity and autonomy the congregations agree to share the services of a minister. With the exception of the manse, about which special terms have to be reached, each congregation keeps its name, its property, its parish, its Kirk Session, its method of managing its temporal affairs. At one time the two Kirk Sessions met together annually to appoint one elder to represent them in Presbytery and

Synod, but in terms of an Act of 1977 each Kirk Session now appoints its own representative elder even although this disturbs the principle of numerical parity of ministers and elders in the superior courts. The two congregations, however, become one charge and it is usual when referring to the charge to call it by the names of the two coupled by the word 'with'.

Temporary or Permanent   A linking may be found to be desirable for either of two reasons. First, that it enables a temporary situation to be taken care of (where, for instance, a union is desirable but not immediately attainable, or where a congregation has to be looked after for a period till some wider readjustment programme emerges) and in such a case it is a temporary linking that will be effected. Such a linking may be effected by the Presbytery with the concurrence of the Edinburgh Committees and it may also be terminated by those same bodies. Secondly, the situation may be that the two congregations are so far apart that they could not conveniently be united but can still be worked by one minister. In such a case the linking will be a permanent one. This is still effected by the Presbytery, but it can be broken only by the Assembly or their Commission.

Manse   It is most important to recognise whether the linking is temporary or permanent when deciding about the manse for the linked charge. Where the linking is of the temporary variety the question of the manse presents peculiar difficulties. It would be very wrong, for example, for one of the manses to be sold and a substantial part of the proceeds used to put the other into good order, since this kind of omelette could not be unscrambled when at some later date it was decided to terminate the linking. That kind of arrangement is, of course, perfectly good in a permanent linking.

Stipend In a case of linking each of the congregations completes a Vacancy Schedule thereby accepting responsibility for an agreed sum as its portion of stipend and ministerial expenses. Each congregation also has a separate allocation in respect of Mission and Service Fund. Provision is often made in the Basis of Linking for an annual joint meeting to discuss financial affairs. In view of the fact that each has its own obligations clearly defined such a meeting has never seemed to me either necessary or desirable.

Basis of Linking The terms of a proposed linking are set forth in a Basis of Linking. This document differs materially from a Basis of Union in that it sets out the conditions of an ongoing association of two existing entities whereas the other makes provision for the creation of an entirely new entity. If, therefore, it is desired to vary the terms of the relationship this may properly be done by having the Basis amended, which seems to call for the consent of the Presbytery and also of the Assembly's Committee.

Delayed Linking Where a linking is considered desirable but is not immediately possible agreement may be reached on a Deferred

Linking. The conditions applying here are exactly as in the case of a Deferred Union described above (p. 85).

Reservation   It should be borne in mind that linking is designed to deal with the situation of two congregations so far apart that they cannot conveniently be united, it is not intended to enable two congregations to remain apart, maintaining independent sets of buildings within a quarter of a mile of one another. There is, surely, something superlatively ridiculous in the spectacle of one group of people in a community on their way from participating in a service at 10 o'clock passing a similar group going to participate in an identical service at 11.30, but in another building situated a hundred yards away.

Nor should too much credence be given to the optimistic suggestion in the Act that linking may be 'a step towards union'. Experience seems to indicate that the opposite is the case and that the fact of linking having worked is taken to prove conclusively that it is just fine to carry on as we are without the need for a closer tie.

5. Transportation

This is defined in the Act as the moving of a congregation 'from one place of worship to another, with or without a change of parish'. It is to be effected by the Synod or by the Commission of Assembly, in either case at the instance of the Presbytery.

I find great difficulty in the bit about no

change of parish. I am myself perfectly clear that a congregation can change from one place of worship to another within its own parish on the authority of the Presbytery and without the intervention of the Synod. Indeed I do not see this as readjustment at all. I take the view, too, that it is misleading to speak of this as 'transportation'.

All that apart, the real significance of the terms from the point of view of practical readjustment has to do with the chance which sometimes emerges of closing down a place of worship in an over-churched district and moving the congregation, with its assets, to a new area altogether. The kind of thing that is in mind is where the site of a church has a very high commercial value, or is the subject of a Compulsory Purchase Order involving the acquiring authority in paying the reasonable cost of equivalent reinstatement, or where there may have been a fire and a large sum of insurance money is available. In such a case it would be most unfortunate to continue or, worse still, to perpetuate the situation of over-churching, and the congregation ought to be encouraged to consider very seriously the possibility of moving with its assets both in finance and in personnel to establish a cause in some Church Extension or similar situation.

6. Terminable Appointment

When it is felt that a congregation should be involved in union but that for the time being this is not practicable then the congregation may be given permission to have a minister appointed on a terminable basis. The official name for this is the 'suppression of the charge' but the term is an unfortunate one and for obvious reasons it is rarely used. It means that the congregation has had taken from it the right to have a minister appointed *ad vitam aut culpam.* That right may, with the concurrence of the Assembly's Committee, be restored by the Presbytery at a later date in view of changed circumstances. If a minister is there when the restoration is effected it will immediately be followed by his induction.

In practical terms the effect of being granted a terminable appointment is that the congregation goes about the search for a minister much as it would do were there no restriction. Having secured a nominee, however, they have simply to come and invite the Presbytery to appoint the person so chosen. In a case of this kind, I take it, the Presbytery has the right, if so advised, to decline to appoint because they consider the nominee unsuitable, whereas in a normal vacancy they have only to assure themselves that the election has been carried through in orderly fashion. I could imagine, too, that there would be people quite unsuitable for appointment in this kind of context.

Specified Period   It is common practice for a definite period of time to be specified: a terminable appointment for a period of three years, for example. It must be made clear that this is a maximum and not a minimum guaranteed period. Neither can the minister be given any guarantee in such a case; the best that can be promised is that the minister will receive, say, three months' notice. If, as has been suggested, the appointment be stated to be for three years that means 'for up to three years'; the appointment will be terminated at the end of three years or on the question of readjustment arising at an earlier time (through a vacancy occurring in a neighbouring parish, for example).

Introduction The nominee, his appointment having been made by the Presbytery, is duly introduced at an appropriate Presbytery service. If he is a minister in a charge he is not translated but demits his charge in order to take up the terminable appointment. If he is a probationer he is, of course, ordained as well as introduced. While he holds the appointment he is a full member of Presbytery, and on the appointment coming to an end if he were otherwise qualified for retirement on account of age or infirmity, he is entitled either to retain a seat in that Presbytery or to return to a seat in the Presbytery of the charge he had demitted to take up the appointment.

7. Restriction

This is the name given to the situation where a congregation is allowed to call a minister *ad vitam aut culpam* but has its choice restricted to a man over a certain age, or to a probationer, or to one whose name appears on the Special List kept by the Assembly's Committee.

There are two reasons either of which may
lead to such a restriction being imposed: first,
that the charge is such that it is felt to be a
necessary one but the work entailed is such in
extent and kind as could be overtaken by an
older man; or, secondly, that it is hoped to
create a situation where the next vacancy may
be expected more or less to coincide with a
vacancy in a neighbouring charge. In the latter
case sometimes permission is given to call a
probationer, the idea being that the charge is
one in which a younger man is unlikely to stay
much longer than five years, though (it should
be added) in this the Presbytery is deliberately
taking a risk since, once inducted, the probationer can stay as long as he cares. The Special
List sounds rather sinister — in fact it contains
the names of men whose translation would
open up a readjustment situation in some
other area.

8. Continued Vacancy

When all efforts at achieving readjustment
have proved fruitless the Presbytery may, with
consent of the Assembly's Committee, declare
the charge a 'continued vacancy'. This means
exactly what it says: no attempt is made to fill
the charge; the interim moderator continues as
moderator of Kirk Session, responsible for
seeing that ordinances are maintained, and the
congregation is served either by a *locum* or by
pulpit supply.

This should never be seen as a long-term

solution but only as a stop-gap arrangement to keep a situation open until some change in the surrounding area opens up further possibilities in the line of readjustment. With this in view the Presbytery should arrange for the position to be reviewed at least once a year. While in many ways it is convenient for a retired minister to act both as interim moderator and as *locum tenens* in a continued vacancy the practice has distinct dangers and is to be discouraged.

9. Reduction

On occasion it may be considered wise to reduce the status of a congregation from that of a full charge to that of a mission station, served, normally, by a lay missionary. A mission station has no constitution of its own, it is under the care of the minister and kirk session of the parish within which it lies, the names of its communicants appear on the roll of the parish church, its missionary works under the direction and control of the parish minister. It is not an independent entity but an integral part of the ecclesiastical structure of the parish as a whole.

I cannot recollect having heard in my time of any case of reduction, and if such were envisaged it could more readily and more properly be achieved simply by effecting a union. Let it be that agreement has been reached that the Church of Auchensnuggle can no longer sustain an independent existence but is prepared to become a mission station under the care of the neighbouring Church at Inversnuggle then it is straightforward for the two congregations to unite, the Basis of Union making provision that Inversnuggle shall be the place of worship but that Auchensnuggle shall be retained as a mission station within the parish. This will automatically take care of members, elders, property, and all the rest.

10. Dissolution

The last resort of all is dissolution. Occasionally, as a result of the depopulation of a parish or other cause, it is found unwise to continue a charge and there is no other with which it is prepared, or it is convenient for it to unite, then it may be thought proper that such a charge should be discontinued completely. There are disadvantages in such a course, and even in a case where it is clear that the members of a gathered congregation intend to scatter there is some advantage in carrying through a form of union with a neighbouring congregation no matter now nominal that union may be. If, however, this is not to be then dissolution is the course to be followed.

The approval of the Unions and Readjustments and Maintenance of the Ministry Committees (and of the Home Board) has to be obtained, and thereafter the matter is taken to the Synod or to the Assembly or their Commission. The Act says that the Presbytery is to 'report' to the Synod and to 'refer' to the

Assembly or the Commission. In my opinion the proper procedure, no matter to which court it goes, is that it should be taken by petition and that at the instance of the Presbytery, with, of course, the concurrence of the various Assembly Committees. In all cases where a lower court is asking a superior court to take some specific action in a matter of particular, rather than of general, interest it does so by petition, and I see no reason to believe that a departure from this universal custom is intended here, no matter how loose the language of the Act may be.

Date of Dissolution   In agreeing to a dissolution the superior court will either itself fix, or will empower the Presbytery to fix, a date for the dissolution to become effective. Since dissolution means 'curtains' in a most irrevocable sense it is most important that the date should be sufficiently delayed not only to permit arrangements to be made for the disposal of the property but also to allow *ex officio* trustees of the congregation to divest themselves of the heritable property. If, for instance, Messrs A and B 'as Clerk of Session and Preses of Managers of the congregation of Roadsend' are vested in the church property then, clearly, once the congregation of Roadsend has ceased to be, their status has gone and they are no longer in a position to give a valid disposition. If delay is envisaged in the final disposal of the buildings (and this is generally to be assumed) then it may be necessary to convey them to a holding body of trustees who will act as individuals. The same people who acted *ex officio* may, if willing, continue to act as individuals, but it is essential that the property should be conveyed to them in their new capacity — by themselves in their old capacity!

Once a decision to seek dissolution has been taken it is most undesirable for the actual ending of the congregation's life to be needlessly protracted. This difficulty can be got over if the Presbytery, at the same time that it resolves to petition at next meeting of Synod (which may be six months away), agree that the Kirk Session be allowed to discontinue services as from an earlier date. In this way the congregation can effectively and with dignity bring its story to a close while still continuing as a legal entity until all necessary formalities have been complied with.

11. Basis of Union

We may now return from this long digression regarding the various possible forms which readjustment may take. We had, it may be recalled, reached the stage where agreement was being arrived at between groups from two congregations about a possibility of union. Let us pick up the story from there.

The next stept is for the Presbytery representatives to draft a Basis of Union or of Linking or of Dissolution if one of these three is envisaged. (If some other form of readjustment is at stake see p. 104). This Basis will set forth the various conditions involved in respect of the name of congregation, property, use of buildings, parish boundaries, ministry, kirk session, temporal management, manse, and any other special considerations.

At this point there may well be a good deal of 'bargaining' between representatives of the conferring congregations. In that context it should be noted in fairness that agreement to a Basis of Union is not the same thing as a vote in favour of a union. An elder may very properly agree that if his congregation is to be united with its neighbour this Basis represents the most fair and equitable arrangement likely to be agreed between the two. He therefore votes in favour of it as a Basis of Union. At the same time, since this represents the most his congregation can get out of such a union he is convinced that its best interests will be served by it remaining independent. He is all set, therefore, to vote against union. In this he is being neither unfair nor inconsistent. It is very necessary, accordingly, for the Presbytery negotiators to ascertain not merely that the local representatives accept the basis but also that they are prepared to recommend agreement to unite in terms of the basis.

Place of Worship The clause likely to cause most heartache is that determining which set of buildings is to be retained. In recent times there has been an increasing willingness to submit this question to arbitration, the congregations committing themselves to the union before the arbiters move in. The Assembly's Committee is prepared to arrange such arbitration. It has much to commend it as a solution of what must necessarily be a difficult problem.

Amending the Basis Agreement having been reached on the terms of a Basis of Union, it is now necessary for this to be taken back to full meetings of office-bearers in each of the conferring congregations. It is important that the Presbytery representatives should be in attendance at such meetings. It may be that at one or other some material change is indicated as being essential if the Basis is to be accepted. If that happens the only thing is for the joint group to meet again to consider this proposal since, obviously, changes cannot be made unilaterally.

Congregational Meetings Now let us imagine that a Basis has been hammered-out which the office-bearers are prepared to recommend for acceptance, or at least are willing to accept as the best Basis that can be mutually agreed. The next step is for the issue to be put to the congregations. This has to be done in each case at a meeting duly called for this purpose by authority of the Presbytery on two Sundays and presided over not by the moderator or interim moderator but by the minister appointed by the Presbytery, being, usually, one of the conferring committee. At the same time that the meetings are being intimated copies of the Basis should be made available for members of the congregation so that they may be studied in advance. There is no provision in Church law whereby this, or any other, issue should be decided by any kind of congregational plebiscite.

In relation to these congregational meetings there are one or two points well worthy of note.

First, that if at all possible the meetings in the two congregations should be held simultaneously, or at least that the one should be held immediately after the other. Considerable harm can be done if an interval is allowed to elapse in which all kinds of highly coloured rumours can circulate in one congregation regarding the reaction of the other. So often in such cases, unfortunately, people's opinions are shaped not by what they themselves think but by what they think other people are thinking.

Secondly, the notice calling the meeting should state the business simply as 'to consider and if so advised to adopt a Basis of Union with the congregation of Other'. This enables the chairman without any ado to rule out of order any extraneous motion. It is not unknown, for example, for someone to make a perfectly proper speech against the union, and then, carried away by his own eloquence and enthusiasm, to go on to declare that the congregation would be far better just to dissolve 'and I beg leave to move that we here and now resolve accordingly'. Nor is it unknown for such a motion to be carried! Dissolution may in fact be the best course, but this is not the way in which it should be dealt with; its implications need to be much more thoroughly explored by the office-bearers who should then submit it to

the congregation with a Basis of Dissolution
attached. To act the other way might be
described as buying a coffin in a poke!

Thirdly, the chairman should go through
the Basis laboriously explaining the clauses one
by one and inviting question and comment. He
should remember that though he has been
wrestling with the document for weeks it is
quite a new set of ideas to most of those
present. He must on no account accept any
proposed amendment to the Basis. If some
point is seen as so important as to involve
rejection, then that should be noted for later
consideration, but the two congregations must
be accepting or rejecting the identical document.

And fourthly, the chairman, after all the
discussion is over, should himself put the
question to the vote: 'Those in favour of
uniting on those terms' and 'Those against'. In
all cases a count should be taken. The chairman
should not call for motions. It is asking a good
deal of even the most convinced office-bearer
to expect him to propose what to many will be
seen as the end of the road for his congregation. But what is far more serious is the risk that
a half-hearted or purely formal motion in
favour will be followed by a real fighting speech
against.

If the vote goes Against in either or both
congregations that is likely to be the end of the
matter, except that in the event that both are
vacant the Presbytery, with concurrence of the
Assembly's Committee, may still proceed to
effect the union or linking.

No Basis Needed

In a case where some form of readjustment is contemplated other than union, linking, or dissolution, there is no Basis and no need to hold a congregational meeting since the decision will be made by the Presbytery with the appropriate concurrence from Edinburgh; that is to say, it is not necessary to have the approval of the congregation for them to be given a restricted ministry. It may well be thought wise, though, to meet with the congregation and let them know what is afoot and to explain the reasons why things are as they are. It is not unlikely that the Presbytery will come in for some hostile criticism at such a gathering, but, on the other hand, people may feel the better for 'getting things off their chest'. In this case one single Sunday's notice is held to be adequate.

Appeal

When the conferring committee makes its final report to the Presbytery with specific proposals with regard to readjustment it is provided that the congregation or congregations concerned should have been cited and may appear at the bar so that they may speak on the proposals and, in the event of the vote going against them, may, if they so desire, appeal to the Synod. It is also laid down that once such an appeal has been taken the Assembly's Committee is to defer consideration of the case until final judgment has been given in the courts.

There, then, are the ramifications of re-adjustment pretty fully examined. Let us now see where you go once you've got permission to proceed.

12. Vacancy procedure

As I say, let's have a look at the details of procedure for filling the vacancy. Unless the contrary is indicated it is assumed that we are dealing with a case where a congregation has been given permission to call without restriction.

Vacancy Declared

It is laid down that 'on the first convenient Sunday' after the occurrence of the vacancy (p. 76) the charge is to be declared vacant. This is done by the interim moderator, and very often he will try to be present in person to do it. It consists simply in reading an intimation to the effect that the charge became vacant on a certain date as a result of whatever the circumstance may have been. If permission to proceed has already been given the intimation may be followed by another intimation about the preparation of the Electoral Register (see hereunder); otherwise it may be added that by order of the Presbytery procedure in the vacancy is meantime sisted.

Time Limit

There is a maximum period of six calendar months allowed to a congregation for the election of a minister, and at the expiry of that time the right of appointment falls to the Presbytery. The point of time from which the period begins is the date when the Assembly's Committee concurs in the Presbytery resolution that the congregation should be allowed to proceed; the date of the *conge d'elire.* The point of time at the other end is the date of appointment, and this I take to be the date when the congregation has duly elected a minister, even although the election has not yet been sustained by the Presbytery. In any case the point is of purely theoretical interest, for Presbyteries generally have no great desire to assume this responsibility and if there seems any hope of the congregation reaching an agreeable solution they will be given the necessary extension of time.

Jus Devolutum This particular piece of legislation, known as the *jus devolutum,* went on the statute-book as part of the Act which abolished patronage, and it was designed to ensure that congregations would act responsibly in the exercise of the new rights that were being conferred upon them. At first the Act was construed very strictly, it being laid down that an extension of time was to be granted only if the congregation had been obstructed or misled by the Presbytery or had been misdirected by the interim moderator. Today it is usual for the Presbytery to grant a three-month extension quite as a matter of form, and to grant a further extension on any reasonable cause shown. Application for extension is supposed to be by petition, but today a letter from the interim moderator is accepted as sufficient.

Presbytery Appointment If after full allowance has been made the congregation still fail to find a minister the duty as well as the right of appointment falls to the Presbytery. The procedure is that the Presbytery having chosen a nominee ascertains that he is prepared to accept, arranges for him to preach in the vacant pulpit, provides a form of Call which members of the congregation are invited to sign, and thereafter adjudicates on the whole situation and, if so advised, confirms the appointment and makes arrangements for the induction, which is as full and final as if the choice had been the congregation's.

There are two reasons principally which lead to a congregation's failure to elect within the prescribed period. The first of these is that there is serious division of opinion within the congregation as to the type of minister for whom they are looking, which can easily lead either to failure to elect or to an election so half-hearted that the man elected feels he cannot accept. It is not necessarily want of enthusiasm; in one case within living memory there was enough 'heat' to lead to the burning of the effigy of the Vacancy Committee Convener in the village square! In such a situation it is often most desirable that the Presbytery should intervene before internal dissension leads to deeper troubles. History shows that many a man appointed in this way (including the effigy case), having made what must be the most inauspicious of starts, has enjoyed a happy and successful and fruitful ministry.

The other reason for failure to elect is that a minister cannot be found prepared to undertake the responsibilities of the charge. Now if the Presbytery is completely satisfied that the charge is a necessary one however discouraging the symptoms then in such a case it is for the Presbytery to convince some suitable minister that he has a duty to consider going. If, on the other hand, the Presbytery has reluctantly agreed to the congregation being given permission to call but its condition is so desolate and its prospects so drear that no-one can be found prepared to undertake a ministry, then I am not at all convinced that the Presbytery has a duty to find a minister. Rather I think they are entitled to raise again the question of readjustment as a consequence of the congregation's failure to find a nominee. The case for your continuing, they would seem to say, was just cogent enough for you to be given the benefit of the doubt; it is certainly not strong enough to justify us in putting it to any man that he has a duty to be your minister.

Electoral Register

The first matter to be attended to is the preparation of an Electoral Register for the congregation, a roll setting forth in alphabetical order the names and addresses of all entitled to vote in the anticipated election, the names being consecutively numbered to avoid the possibility of interpolations or erasures. To this Register, once it has been finally made up and attested, a name cannot be added for any reason whatever, and from it a name can be deleted only on death or on the issue of a disjunction certificate, which must have been asked for by letter. The preparation of the Register may proceed in spite of the fact that the question of readjustment has been raised.

Register Made Up Intimation is given that the Kirk Session is appointed to meet on a specified day at a certain hour to make up the Register, which will contain the names of all on the Communion Roll (not those on the Supplementary Roll) and also the names of persons who give in Certificates of Transference before the date of the meeting. The Session will at the same time receive and adjudge claims to be put on the Register as Adherents, that is, regular worshippers in the congregation, not being members of any other congregation. Against a decision of the Kirk Session to be registered as an Adherent there is no right of appeal.

Inspection of Register The Register having thus been prepared is made available for inspection on a couple of Sundays and at such other times and places as may be thought proper. Thereafter the Kirk Session will meet to consider any claims arising out of the inspection and will finally make up the Register which will be attested by the interim moderator and the Clerk and later by the Clerk of Presbytery. Intimation of this meeting is made on two Sundays.

Election of Vacancy Committee

If permission to call has been given, on the same days as the two intimations are made about the inspection of the Register a further intimation should be made that a meeting of the congregation is to be held for the purpose of electing a Vacancy Committee and of determining the method of election of a Minister. Nowadays this meeting is almost invariably held at the close of a Sunday service. The Vacancy Committee is the body which will search around for a nominee or nominees for filling the vacancy. Although its official title is Congregational Committee I see no reason to depart from the title Vacancy Committee which is the term in universal use.

How Many?   The first thing to be done after the constitution of the meeting by the interim moderator (the Session Clerk acting as Clerk) is to decide on the size of the Committee. It is recommended that the following maxima should not be exceeded: thirteen for a congregation up to 500, nineteen for up to 1000, and twenty-five for more than that.

Who Are Eligible?   Anyone whose name appears on the Electoral Register (member or adherent) is eligible to act on the Vacancy Committee. It is desirable that in choosing the Committee the congregation should seek to ensure that it will be as widely representative a body as possible, reflecting all interests: youth and age, Session and Guild, organisations, ordinary membership, *etc*; all should so far as practicable have a voice. It is important too to remember that their duties will take members of the Committee away on many Sundays and that the home front must not be denuded of responsible office-bearers.

How Elected? The method of electing the Committee is by nomination followed by standing to be counted. Reference should be made to the section on the election of elders (p. 4) for the procedure is the same.

Once persons to the appropriate number have been elected the interim moderator should read over their names and should intimate a date for a first meeting, which may very conveniently be at the close of the congregational meeting since only formal business is likely to be involved at this stage.

Method of Election of Minister

There is a second item of business for this congregational meeting, and it must not be overlooked, that is, to decide upon the method to be followed in the election of the minister, whether it shall be by ballot or by open vote. This is a question which has got to be answered at this point, and the decision cannot subsequently be altered. I remember a case where, the meeting having decided upon ballot, a minister was in due course elected by popular acclamation on the day when he preached as sole nominee. A member of the congregation complained to Presbytery about the irregularity and it was ordained that a ballot election would have to be held. Apart from upsetting the arrangements that had been made for the induction this did no great harm for there was an equally enthusiastic ballot vote. But the possibilities of real trouble were there.

As is explained hereunder (p. 121) there are cases where a ballot vote is necessary, but in most cases today an open vote of the congregation is considered appropriate.

The Vacancy Committee appointed and the method of election determined all that remains for the interim moderator is to close the meeting.

Who May be Called?

This may be a convenient point at which to note what classes of people are eligible for nomination by the Vacancy Committee. Particulars of these are set forth in much fuller detail in Act I of 1977, and the terms of this Act should be carefully studied before the nomination of anyone other than a minister in a charge or a probationer. What follows is stated in fairly general terms.

Ministers in Charges Any minister in a charge in the Church of Scotland is available, with this single exception: a man in his first charge can be nominated only if he has completed five years in that charge or if the interim moderator has obtained from the Presbytery Clerk concerned a certificate stating that there are exceptional circumstances that would justify the minister's going earlier. It should be noted that the five years must have been completed by the date of nomination, not the anticipated date of settlement; that it is a first charge of a parish and that other kinds of appointment do not count; and that the onus for obtaining such a certificate lies with the interim moderator and that it has to be got before nomination and not after election.

Outwith the Service of the Church A minister who has taken up an appointment outwith the control of the Church may be called to a vacant charge provided he has made arrangements for resigning from that appointment and has received a certificate from the Committee on Admission of Ministers as to his status and character.

Other Presbyterian Churches Again in general terms any minister of a charge in the Presbyterian Church of Ireland or in the United Reformed Church in England and Wales is eligible, provided he can produce the necessary certificates from his own Church — which includes a reference to the course of training he has undergone.

Probationers A probationer may preach as a nominee in a vacancy only with consent of the Committee on Probationers. A probationer who is still serving his probationary year may be invited to be nominated for a charge, but the actual nomination must await the approval of his 'year' by the Committee on Education for the Ministry.

Restricted Call In cases where permission has been given to call only within a restricted group it is of course necessary for the Committee to confine themselves to people who conform to the restrictions. If, for example, they

are confined to men over fifty-five there is no
point in coming to the Presbytery to say that Mr
Old is already fifty-three and remorselessly
growing older, and would not he do fine? He'll
be fifty-five in next to no time! There can be
only one answer, and disappointment of this
sort is best avoided by confining the choice to
those who clearly conform to the conditions.

Task of the Vacancy Committee

At its first meeting the Vacancy Committee
appoints a Convener and a Clerk, and possibly
also a Vice-Convener. The interim moderator
sits with the Vacancy Committee as an assessor
available to offer advice and guidance. He may
if thought appropriate be invited, and may
agree, to act as Convener, but even if he does
this he has no vote, either deliberative or
casting.

Preaching Leet   The Committee will take an
early opportunity to consider the method by
which it is going to proceed. Very likely it will
decide to seek a sole nominee for submission to
the congregation. It is not bound to do this and
may, if so minded, decide to put up the names
of two or more people to preach as a leet before
the whole congregation. This, I am happy to
say, is rarely done nowadays, and I doubt
whether, in the present situation of shortage,
many ministers would be prepared to take part
in the kind of preaching competition which this
involves.

List Available   A list of ministers desirous of
change and a list of probationers available for

call may be had on application to the Committee on Probationers and Transference of Ministers. It is most important to note, as has already been said, that if a probationer is being considered this ought to be 'cleared' with that same Committee as early as possible.

Advertisement It may be decided to advertise the vacancy in the press, and if this is done care must be exercised not to make statements about stipend, *etc.*, which have not been agreed with the Presbytery and the Assembly's Committee on the Maintenance of the Ministry. There is in some quarters a measure of prejudice against the whole idea of advertising, it being felt that in the calling of a minister to a vacant charge the initiative should lie at a higher level than the columns of the daily press. To such people indeed the whole idea of application is repugnant as being in conflict with the working of the Holy Spirit. This may be so, but I am sure it is no more so than is the system of whispering to someone that he might speak to someone who, it is understood, knows someone. . . . And this is one of the alternative methods that seems to be acceptable. An application has at least an element of directness and openness which the other signally lacks.

Reading between the Lines Where a man submits an application (whether in answer to an advertisement or not) the discriminating reader can glean a great deal from the document itself beyond what it actually says; the man who is slapdash about this is liable to be careless about most things, the man who makes a parade here will do the same in other circumstances also, the tone of the application has its own significance, and so on. I have seen applications which seemed to me to say — indeed to shout — 'I have lots of qualifications and am keen to come to you, but you'd be well advised to look elsewhere.' The daddy o' them a' in my experience was the case of the man who submitted a stencilled form of application with the blanks filled in by hand: 'I hereby make application for the vacant parish of . . . I am . . . years of age, married, and have . . . children. I have been . . . years in my present charge' and so it went on. Could he possibly have devised a formula for saying more emphatically, 'For many years now I have been applying unsuccessfully for vacancies, and I expect to be doing so for a long time to come. But I suppose there's always a chance that you might be interested.'

Enquiry Most members of any Vacancy Committee are likely to have connections with church-going people in different parts of the country and to that extent are in the way of hearing of ministers suitable to their vacancy. If only people would put their minds to it this can be one of the most helpful ways of getting on the track of a likely man. For in spite of what I have said in favour of advertising, the person likely to reply to such an advertisement is the person who has moving in mind, for some reason, whereas it may well be that the person best suited to your needs is perfectly happy where he is and has no thought of a change. It

would never occur to him to apply for your
vacancy, but if he were presented quite spon-
taneously with an invitation to come it would be
a horse of a totally different colour. But don't
disturb people in this situation unless you are
quite seriously interested.

Going on Tour   In due course the Committee will no doubt find itself dividing up into
small visiting sub-committees going hither and
thither to see and hear and assess possible
nominees. This they should try to do as quietly
and tactfully as possible, bearing in mind the
ongoing ministry of the man and the parish.
For a carload of strangers to disembark at the
Church door, to enquire of the duty-elder
whether there are special seats for visitors, to
stand around in a huddle afterwards in solemn
conclave — for this to happen is bound to set
tongues awagging in even the most lethargic
country parish. And all this may have occurred
although the man had not applied, indeed was
not being considered by the Vacancy Committee at all, but one of the groups had a free
Sunday, it was a nice day, and there was a car
available!

Interview   It may be that the Committee,
once seriously interested in some candidate,
will wish to have a talk with him. This is a
perfectly reasonable desire. The Committee
should remember, however, the limits of prop-
riety in any such interview, that though he may
be 'assisting them with their enquiries' he is not
a suspect, and they would particularly be wise
to bear in mind that they are probably reveal-

ing far more about themselves than they are eliciting from the minister interviewed. They should be at pains to ensure that what they do so reveal will be such as to make the man feel he wants to be their minister. Many a likely minister has been put off by the interview.

Expenses When a minister from a remote part of the country indicates a willingness to make himself 'audible' somewhere to suit their convenience it should not be assumed by the Committee that he is prepared to do so at his own expense; even if he were he should not be allowed to do this. He himself may hesitate to mention the matter of his outlays when he is being 'interviewed' for fear he should give the impression of being 'the money-grubbing sort,' but the Committee should be at pains to discover the extent of these outlays and should refund them. It's not fair to ask, 'Did you have any expenses?' as though men normally got from Caithness to Cowdenbeath without being out-of-pocket. Or, worse still, there's the technique of gently advancing an envelope with the words, 'We always offer to pay expenses but,' drawing the envelope back, 'they never take them.' Whether or not the man is to be further considered is irrelevant so far as this kind of blackmail is concerned.

Finding a Nominee Usually ere long a name emerges of one who has captured the fancy of the bulk of the Committee and steps can then be taken to approach that person and make arrangements for him to be officially nominated.

On occasion, on the other hand, there may be marked division in the Committee as between two men characterised by two entirely different sets of qualification. Probably on a vote one of these would come up with a slender majority and could therefore be put forward as sole nominee. Before taking this step, though, it is well to consider the position carefully. For it is likely that the division in the Committee will be reflected in the congregation itself and will result in a significant split in the vote. Now in such a case the congregation is not so much voting For or Against the sole nominee as rather For the sole nominee or For some unsuccessful nominee about whom they have heard on the grape-vine. The trouble is that while Smith can readily accept appointment in an election where he had 300 votes against 200 for Brown, it's not at all so easy to accept appointment when the voting has been 300 For and 200 Against.

When a Vacancy Committee has got to this stage the wisest course may be for them to drop both candidates and start afresh. Things may even have reached the stage where they should call a congregational meeting (through the Kirk Session) and report failure to nominate and ask for the appointment of a new Vacancy Committee.

Precautions It is important that before being asked finally to accept nomination a candidate should have the opportunity of seeing over the church and halls as well as the manse, and also the manse garden. In the case of a congregation administered under the former U.P. constitution it is required by law that he be shown a copy of the constitution in current use. Once a nomination has been made public it is important that, unless for some very compelling reason, the election should go forward. For one thing it will have attracted some publicity, and if it is turned down the Committee will find itself in a most awkward position in relation to approaching anyone else on the list, so very often they have to start again from the very beginning. As far as possible, therefore, it should be ascertained that the candidate is likely to accept before the Committee comes out into the open with a name.

Election Immediately the Committee has decided upon a sole nominee it has first of all to obtain his consent in writing and then to report the situation to the Kirk Session in the form of a duly certified Minute delivered to the interim moderator.

Although the Act says nothing about it, the invariable practice is that arrangements are made for the nominee to conduct public worship on the first convenient Sunday. If it has been decided that the election shall be by open vote the meeting for the purpose of electing will probably be held at the close of such service. Two Sundays' notice are of course given of this meeting. The interim moderator shall preside and put the simple question, 'Elect Mr So-and-so — or Not?' Tellers should be appointed and a count taken no matter how unanimous the vote may be. The moderator shall then declare the result of the voting, and, if appropriate, shall go on to declare Mr So-and-so has been elected 'subject to the judgment of the courts of the Church'.

Election by Ballot A ballot-vote is, naturally, rather more complicated than the other and is little resorted to today except in certain cases where it is essential that it be done this way. For instance in a linked charge where the nominee has to conduct services in two separate places of worship, or in a deferred union where two distinct congregations are involved (though here it may well be possible, and is desirable, to arrange for one preaching and one election). Where in a straightforward case it is desired that the nominee shall preach in the evening as well as the morning an immediate open election is not possible and a ballot may be resorted to. In the case of a linked charge the ballot papers should be put together and mixed before counting so that the preponderance of voting in each congregation may not be disclosed.

It is for the interim moderator to arrange facilities for voting both during some part of the day and in the evening. He shall himself be present and may invoke the aid of another minister. Ballot papers prepared in advance shall be available, and one shall be issued to each voter on presenting himself, provided his name appears on the Electoral Register.

Counting the Votes As soon as possible, usually immediately the voting closes and certainly not later than the next day, the Kirk

Session shall be constituted, and in presence of the elders the interim moderator and his ministerial assistant shall duly count the votes. Once this has been done the moderator shall issue a declaration of the result, and a copy of this shall immediately be affixed to the door (or notice-board) of the Church. The moderator shall cause further intimation to be made from the pulpit on the next Sunday. Voting papers and counterfoils shall go to the Presbytery Clerk along with the other papers and, after the settlement has been completed, shall be destroyed by him.

The Call

The next business is to have a Call prepared. Today when mostly we are dealing with cases of sole nomination and open election the Call is something of a duplication and even a superfluity. It may be asked that if five hundred out of a congregation of eight hundred have turned out to hear and have unanimously elected a minister, what more proof does he need of their satisfaction with him and their desire to have him as their minister?

It is important to understand something of the history of this ancient institution, the Call. It dates from the day of patronage when the congregation had no say in choosing their minister who was presented by the patron, and the Call represented their only response, their sole chance of welcoming the presentee and promising him their loyalty. From the minister's point of view this was not unimportant, for although the law did not require the congregation to concur in his appointment he himself may well have taken the position that he would accept only if he had reason to believe that the congregation would be with him.

After patronage had gone and the preaching competition had become the order of the day the Call still had a significant place, for it enabled me to say to Mr Smith, the successful candidate, that though I had cast my vote in favour of Mr Brown yet I was prepared wholeheartedly to accept the will of the majority and to give my unstinted support to the successful man.

Arrangements for Signing   It is the responsibility of the Kirk Session to make arrangements for the signing of the Call as well as for the election. When the election is by open vote the simple plan is to have plenty of call-sheets, tables, and pens available and to try to secure the signatures of all the voters before they leave. This really means 'plenty'; otherwise people will slink away 'to get the potatoes on' rather than form an orderly queue. The Call can then be available for a couple more Sundays and also at specified times and places during week-days, though in the latter case it must always be in the care of a member of Kirk Session.

When a ballot-vote has been resorted to it is not so easy, since obviously nothing can be done about signing the Call until the result of the election has been declared. I remember a case, though, when a Call was produced to the

Presbytery the very next day after a ballot vote had been held. On enquiry of the interim moderator (a Highlandman) I discovered that the voters, having completed in conditions of great secrecy a ballot paper asking Yes or No, had then been confronted with a demand to sign Yes on a Call-sheet. The interim moderator did not see any incongruity. Maybe, of course, it sounded different in the Gaelic!

Number of Signatures At least eight days must be allowed for signing the Call, but in case of urgency the papers may be taken to the Presbytery immediately after the election, with a request in name of the Kirk Session that the Call be returned for further signatures. Or the Presbytery itself, if it is not satisfied that the Call reflects sufficient enthusiasm, may return it to the Kirk Session to have it further signed. This is always a difficult one, for if the level of zest within the congregation has fallen so low that folk are not interested even to sign the Call then the logical conclusion seems to be that they are desperately needing a settled ministry and that no useful purpose is going to be served by delaying the induction. In any case it is specifically forbidden to canvass the Call, so it's hard to see what the Kirk Session can do about it.

Mandate A member unable to attend and sign the Call in person may complete a Form of Mandate which will be supplied by the Session Clerk, and on this being presented, the Elder in attendance will write the name on to the

Call-sheet, authenticating it with his own initials.

Paper of Concurrence Only those can sign the Call whose names appear on the Electoral Register, but a further document called a Paper of Concurrence may be signed by others, these being persons over fourteen years of age who are connected with the congregation. These may be called 'adherents' but not in the same sense as those whose names appear on the Electoral Register as such and who are entitled to sign the Call proper.

Financial Arrangements

While all this activity has been progressing at the instance of the Vacancy Committee and latterly of the Kirk Session, the financial court should not have been idle. Following immediately upon the resolution of the readjustment situation a Vacancy Schedule will have been issued to the treasurer, and this, in conference with Presbytery representatives, should have been completed and submitted to the Presbytery, which, if satisfied, will have transmitted it to the Assembly's Committee.

The Presbytery is not supposed to deal with an appointment and call unless this matter of the stipend arrangements has been completed and the clerk has a Minute of the Assembly's Committee in his hand. Most emphatically an induction must not take place before this has all been attended to. Among the papers which the Presbytery Clerk will hand to the minister on his induction is a Minute setting forth clearly what these stipend arrangements are.

Sustaining the Election and Call

All is now ready for proceeding to the Presbytery.

Lodging the Papers The papers, which ought to be in the hands of the Presbytery Clerk some days before the meeting, include all formal intimations that have been read from the pulpit, the voting papers and counterfoils in the case of a ballot, the Call itself with an indication of the number of signatures, and in the case of anyone other than a minister in a charge the necessary certificates as to status and eligibility. There must also be a letter from the person elected indicating acceptance and containing an assurance that he has used no undue influence by himself or others to secure the Call. This assurance is still regarded as vitally important today although it seems to me to be something of an anachronism. It represents all that is left of the Act on Simoniacal Practices which was directed against 'the great danger which may arise to this Church from Bargaining betwixt titulars or tacksmen of teinds or heritors or members or adherents in parishes on the one hand, and candidates for the ministry or friends of such candidates on the other'. No-one would call it a live issue today.

At the Presbytery The clerk will arrange for the matter to come before the first meeting of the court and will see that an edict is read citing the calling congregation to this meeting for their interest. The congregation ought to meet, however briefly, to appoint commissioners to 'prosecute the Call before the Presbytery'.

The Presbytery having considered the relevant documents and heard the commissioners will then decide whether or not to sustain the election and call. If the call be addressed to a minister in another charge the Presbytery will also either appoint commissioners to prosecute the call before the other Presbytery involved (and these need not be members of Presbytery) or, which is today much more common, may instruct the clerk to forward the papers to the clerk of the other Presbytery. It will also make arrangements, provisional if another Presbytery is involved, for the induction (or ordination and induction) of the person appointed. This judgment will be conveyed by the moderator to the commissioners attending from the congregation.

At the Receiving End At the expense of interrupting the story for a moment, it will be convenient at this point to indicate briefly the situation that is created at the receiving end, that is, where a minister has a Call addressed to him. Normally he will have informed first his office-bearers and then his congregation as soon as he has accepted nomination. By that time the fact of his interest can be counted upon to have become public, and it is most desirable that his people should first hear from himself of his impending departure.

Once he has been elected and arrangements

made for the Call to be dealt with by the calling Presbytery, the clerk of his own Presbytery should be consulted so that arrangements can be put in hand timeously. First of all an interim moderator has to be found, and while this appointment is made by the Presbytery it is usual to listen sympathetically to any suggestion the Kirk Session has to offer as to a suitable and acceptable person. A neighbour is an obvious choice, but it must be equally apparent that a neighbour whose congregation is likely to be involved with the vacant congregation in readjustment negotiations should certainly not be chosen.

The congregation has to be cited to the meeting of Presbytery at which the translation is to be considered. An intimation to this effect is sent by the Presbytery Clerk and requires to be made on only one Sunday. A congregational meeting is held at the close of public worship, presided over preferably by the prospective interim moderator, and commissioners are appointed to attend the Presbytery meeting when they will be heard. Once on a time it was common to plead that a man should not be translated. Today it is recognised that if he has made up his mind he ought to go no useful purpose will be served by putting obstacles in his way. Most congregations, therefore, 'reluctantly concur' in the loss of their minister or, at least, that's how they generally express it!

Induction

At the meeting when it fixes the time for the

induction the Presbytery also appoints a meeting *in hunc effectum* for, say, a quarter of an hour before the time of the Service for the purpose of dealing with any objections which may be made to the life or doctrine of the inductee. An edict is sent to the interim moderator by the Presbytery Clerk calling for such objections, and this is to be returned on or before the day of the induction attested as having been read on two Sundays and no objections having been received. The comments made on page 7 in regard to the ordination of elders are relevant here.

Further Citation When the Presbytery has been constituted it may be necessary to begin by reporting that the other Presbytery concerned has concurred in the Call and has agreed to translate. The edict is then laid on the table. Further intimation is now made that the Presbytery is in session and is prepared to receive objections. Today, I think, this is invariably done by reading the edict once again in face of the congregation, but the tradition is that it should be read 'at the most patent door of the Church'. Whatever the practical limitations of this old system its symbolism is certainly right, for it is a reminder to both pulpit and pew that a minister is being inducted to the parish and not just to the congregation, and that this is an event of as much significance to the careless and the inattentive out yonder as it is to the faithful gathered within.

Notice of Induction After the Service of Induction the Presbytery resumes its session when the name of the new minister is added to the Roll of Presbytery and the interim moderator is thanked and discharged. A certified intimation of induction is supplied by the Presbytery Clerk and conveyed to the Clerk of Session who engrosses it in the first Minute of a Session meeting thereafter.

New Chapter Begins

And so a new ministry has begun, you have reached the end of your vacancy and your congregation is now 'full' once more. If I mistake not you are probably at this point issuing a large sigh of relief and hoping you won't have it all to go through again for a long time.

A Glossary of Terms Used

Appropriate Stipend — the stipend agreed by the Presbytery in consultation with the General Assembly's Committee on the Maintenance of the Ministry as the proper stipend to be paid to the minister of that charge.

conge d'élire — permission to choose a minister.

de die in diem — from day to day — appointment on a terminable basis.

Demission — resignation by a minister of his charge — which to become effective must be accepted by the Presbytery.

Edict — public intimation read from the pulpit.

ex officio — in virtue of the office held.

Formula, The — form of words subscribed to by all admitted to any office in the Church. It is as follows:

> I believe the fundamental doctrines of the Christian Faith contained in the Confession of Faith of this Church.
> I acknowledge the Presbyterian government of this Church to be agreeable to the Word of God, and promise that I will submit thereto and concur therewith.
> I promise to observe the order of worship and the administration of all public ordinances as the same are or may be allowed in this Church

Heritors — owners of heritable property in a parish (see page 38).

Induction *ad vitam aut culpam* — admission as minister of a charge for life or until fault.

Introduction — admission to a position on a *de die in diem* basis.

jus devolutum — a right of appointment to a charge devolving on the Presbytery because it has not been timeously exercised by the congregation.

Listed Expenses — six kinds of ministerial expenses to be paid for or on behalf of a minister and not included in stipend.

Oath *de fideli* (*administratione officii*) — oath taken by all undertaking special office within the courts: 'I promise that I will carry out faithfully the duties of. . . .'

Prima facie — on the face of things.

quoad omnia — in respect of all matters (see page 36).

quoad sacra — in respect of sacred matters (see page 36).

Sist procedure — to stop it in the meantime.

Teind — (the traditional 'tenth' or 'tithe') a charge upon the fruits of the land payable to the minister by the heritors.

Translation — the movement of a minister from one parish to another.